# MOMS are from MARS

### a savory blend of memories, opinions, advice and ridiculousness

### by
### Janene Murphy

Copyright © 2013 by Janene Murphy

All rights reserved. No part of this book may be reproduced or transmitted in any form or by any electronic or mechanical means, including photocopying, recording or by any information storage and retrieval system, without the written permission of the publisher, except where permitted by law.

Some of the material in this book originally appeared, occasionally in different form, in the blog Moms are from Mars (http://momsarefrommars.com)

This is not a work of fiction, still the author is a little addled in the brain. Some events may not have happened exactly as they appear in this book. Also, many names have been changed to protect the innocent as well as the guilty.

The author acknowledges the trademarked status and trademark owners of various products referenced in this work of fiction, which have been used without permission. The publication of these trademarks is associated with or sponsored by the trademark owners.

ISBN-13: 978-1484819005
ISBN-10: 1484819004

# Table of Contents

Getting started....................................................................5

Chapter One: Let There Be Abs ......................................13

Chapter Two: People Be Crazy.......................................28

Chapter Three: Motherhood Sucks, Part One - Let's Get Physical..42

Chapter Four: Motherhood Sucks, Part Two - Emotion Sickness....58

Chapter Five: There's Something Wrong with Me .........75

Chapter Six: Lost in Translation.....................................91

Chapter Seven: If You Are What You Wear, I'm Sunk................112

Chapter Eight: Bringing Home the Bacon.....................130

Chapter Nine: Insecurity Blanket...................................145

Chapter Ten: Make Good Choices!................................158

Chapter Eleven: Vacation Frustration............................179

Photo Credits.................................................................196

Acknowledgments..........................................................197

About the Author...........................................................198

**MOMS are from MARS**

*About this book…*

If you are here because you're familiar with my website and blog, *Moms are from Mars,* that is awesome. If you're not, however, don't worry. I forgive you. Still, there are some things you should know. First off, I'm a little weird. Or maybe just honest. I'll let you be the judge. All I know is my experiences as a child, teen, young adult and world traveler have sort of, well, warped me. As for being a mother, all I can say is nothing in the world prepared me for such a crazy job.

What you'll find in these pages is a glorious combination of blog posts and original content. They'll feature tales from my life, sage advice, as well as many of my not so humble opinions. I'll admit you will also come across some bouts of craziness. What can I say? Humor is my number one coping mechanism and I've coped with a lot.

So if you're interested in reading an intelligent soul's astute observations of the world, put this book down now. But if you're interested in the ramblings of a woman who admits she's not quite normal, read on.

Now let's begin…

Oops!

Wait a second. Before I start, there are a few caveats. First off, my use of pictures. If you're a fan of my blog you may notice there aren't as many photographs in this book. During the formatting process, photos are kind of a pain and I'm not exactly tech savvy. Plus, if you're reading this as an ebook, you know pictures take up a lot of storage space. I'd hate for you to delete this book to make room for your quarterly issue of *Miniature Donkey Talk* magazine. (And, yes, that is a real magazine. Some things I just can't make up.) Never fear, though. When it comes to photographs I will do one of three things: 1) just use the dang photo -- including exclusive ones that can't be found on my blog, 2) alter my words slightly so they don't refer to original pictures found in my posts or 3) use my tremendous writing skills to provide powerful imagery, thereby allowing you to visualize the aforementioned photo in your head.

Let's practice the last strategy with a couple of examples. Instead of showing you this:

I will write, "a sweet brown baby bunny sitting atop a soft bed of straw as it nibbles away at a succulent pile of hot pink flower petals." And instead of showing you this:

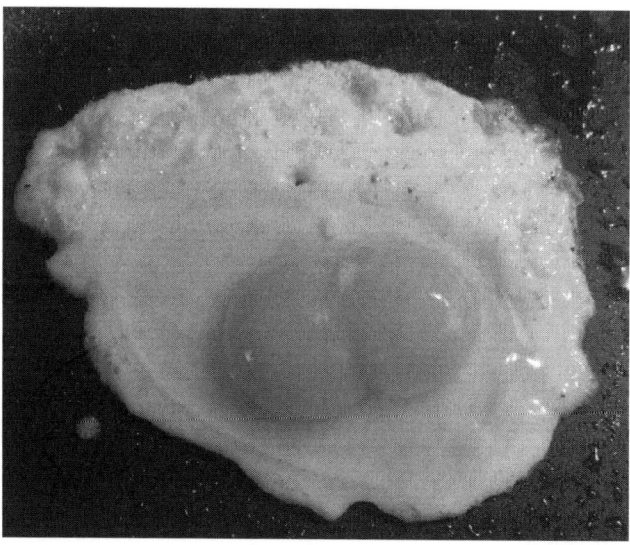

I will write, "a butt egg." Please note, though, if the situation *does* call for a photo of a butt egg I will use it. Some things just can't be substituted.

Will that work for you? I hope so, since this book is already in your hands. But if it doesn't work, feel free to grab a fruit-flavored lollipop and suck it to your heart's delight.

By the way, if you find the phrase *suck it* offensive, let it be known this is the first and only time I will use it. Actually, that's not true. I will use it one more time to discuss an old boyfriend but that's only because he was a real frickin' jerk.

(Side note: The word *frickin'* will be used periodically as it gives people the impression that I'm street. Though, let's be honest. The fact that I'm a white, forty-something mom from Iowa should be proof enough of that already.)

All right. I've covered the issues of photos and language, which leaves only one more thing. Every once in a while you will experience a **ViOLeNT aCT of RaNDoMNeSS**. These will be stories or errant blog posts which, to be completely honest, have no business being in this book. This, of course, means I have to include them. Like I said, I'm kind of weird. Please note when I first put this book together, I inserted them in the middle of chapters to go for that truly random effect. But I found when I re-read this book, they induced a rage in me which could not be quelled without medical intervention. So instead all acts of randomness -- save one -- will be found at the end of each chapter. I know that doesn't exactly make them random but I like the name so I'm keeping it. As for the one act that *won't* be found after a chapter, I decided it would interrupt...

# ViOLeNT aCT of RaNDoMNeSS!

### *Marathon Madness!* -- *January 19, 2012*
**Confession:** I haven't worked out in over two months. I blame bad knees and a slow-healing ankle. As a result, my body looks like a Jello jiggler. Something must be done.

But what? I tried to think of something big and bold, something that would make a statement. Then it came to me. For the first time in my life, I'm going to participate in a marathon.

It's a big step, I know and I'm really nervous. Truth be told, I'm not sure I can do it. Still, I think I've found the perfect one for me: *iCarly's* **"Great Gobs of Gibby" marathon on Nickelodeon.**

I know what you're thinking: That's so lame. Why not *The Wizards of Waverly Place* instead? Believe me, I thought about that, too, but I've got to start out slow. *iCarly's* lack of character development and story arcs make for an easy, even course. The last thing I want to do is sprain an eyelash my first time out of the box. Plus I never did find out what happened after Sam kissed Freddy in last year's season finale. I've lost way too much sleep over it. It's time to end the madness.

The training starts now. I've got fourteen episodes lined up on my TiVo. Today, I'll watch one show. Tomorrow, two. Before you know it, I'll be ready. As for carbo-loading? Don't you worry. I'm a pro at that. I just bought the Frito-Lay Classic Mix bag featuring not one, but TWO types of Doritos! All I need now is a blueberry cheesecake, a case of Yoo-hoo and I'm good to go.

So wish me luck. I know I'm going to need it. Reliving Carly's bedroom fire will be tough. But I'll do it in the name of marathon participants everywhere.

Hopefully, I'll make them proud.

See? That was kind of disruptive, wasn't it? Regardless, it is time to start this book. There will be no more interruptions or silliness. I promise.

The book begins *now*.

**MOMS are from MARS**

This page intentionally left blank

*...just to mess with you.*

**MOMS are from MARS**

# CHAPTER ONE
## Let There Be Abs

February 18th is a big day in history. In 1846, it marked the start of the Galician peasant revolt. More importantly, in 1930, Elm Farm Ollie became the first cow to fly in an airplane. Now that's progress. In 1968, Molly Ringwald was born. In 1974, Kiss released its first album. It's also the day my first blog post was published. The year: 2010.

A lot led up to the launch of my website. From the time I was a tot, I loved to tell stories. I loved writing them, too, but didn't seriously put pen to paper until I was thirty-nine years old. I sent my first manuscript to five million literary agents. None showed any interest. The next book I wrote went to three agents. One took me on. I couldn't believe my luck.

"You need to build an audience," my agent said as he shopped my book around. "Why don't you start a blog?" Following instructions, I did. The guy dumped me three months later. Perhaps he wasn't a fan.

But don't cry for me, Argentina. My motto is the same as my blood type: be positive (B+). I found I loved the blogging business. Plus people listened to me, something my kids had never done. I found my audience wasn't just teenaged girls, either, as I had originally intended. Still, when I sat down to write my first post, I did have a teen girl audience in mind. I knew I had to compose something special -- something with heart, soul, tremendous insight...and abs.

You heard me. Rock hard abs. They always capture people's attention and, at the time, Taylor Lautner's were getting plenty. Armed with that knowledge, a laptop, and a dash of over-confidence, I wrote my first post.

**EIGHT PACK VS. EIGHT TRACK**

In an effort to explain strange mom behavior, I illustrated the differences between teen idols of yesterday and today. What prompted this? That November some friends and I had gone to see the latest Twilight movie, *New Moon*. The experience left me more than a little unsettled.

We'd gone to an 11 AM showing on a Friday afternoon. It had been a school day, so there were few teens in the crowd. The large majority had been moms like us, ones who shared a love for the vampire series. Imagine my horror when Taylor Lautner took off his shirt and half the middle-aged audience shrieked in delight. Sure, the boy was hot --beefcake at its finest -- but, jeez, he'd just turned eighteen!

Anyway, as we were leaving the theater my friends and I discussed the movie -- the plot, some key scenes and, of course, Jacob's abs. "Man," one said. "He didn't have a six-pack. He had an eight-pack!" Indeed. Then another chimed in, "When we were growing up, we never had teen idols like that."

And we didn't. Oh, boy, we didn't. I have to say I was a little jealous. In fact, I still am today. My teen idol growing up was Shaun Cassidy. I loved listening to his 8-track tapes (this was *way* before iPods) and didn't miss one episode of *The Hardy Boys* TV show. As a matter of fact, one of my darkest moments involved a pink satin baseball jacket with Shaun's hot n' handsome image silk screened on the back. My mom said I couldn't have it despite how beautiful it looked on the Sear's store mannequin. Tragic.

Now in typical teen idol fashion, Shaun Cassidy was totally gorgeous. But his bod was so skinny you could thread a needle with him. Other teen idols were like him, too -- Leif Garrett, Scott Baio, and Andy Gibb. All of them had dreamy eyes, fabulous hair, and chests as flat as Brownie Girl Scouts.

So how do the teen idols of yesterday relate to the present day situation? I'm not sure, but if kids catch their moms gaping at a magazine spread of Taylor "Eight-Pack" Lautner in the check out aisle at the Piggly Wiggly, they should take pity on her. If, however, she squeals when teenaged actors take their shirts off in a movie, the kids have permission to disown her.

### CRUSHED

Ah, boys. They played a huge role in my imaginary love life while I was growing up. I had my first crush while in the second grade. His name was Brian. He was tall and didn't eat his boogers. Other than those two facts I knew very little about him, primarily because we never spoke. If he'd had a crazy obsession with Bonnie

Bell Lip Smackers, I never knew. I'm glad. That would have been really gross.

I still remember the day my parents found one of the numerous love letters I had written to him. Of course, none had ever been sent. Outside of the obvious fear factor, I didn't have cool personal stationary *like every other girl in school whose parents loved them more than my parents loved me.* How could I adequately express my love on a torn out piece of notebook paper? Anyway, the letter started off with a bang. "Dear Brain," it said. Yep, Brain instead of Brian. Go ahead and laugh. I never said I had been a good speller. In my defense, though, Brian was very smart. Dare I say a brain? Still, when my parents read that opening salutation they chuckled, sending me into a rage. This was love! How dare they mock my tender feelings! Mike and Carol Brady would never have done that.

As with much young love, after the discovery of that letter, my feelings for Brian quickly faded. I couldn't handle the humiliation. Instead, I focused my attention on spelling. Here is the result:

superkalafragalisticexpialidosius

That's right, Mom and Dad. I learned to spell the melodious word from *Mary Poppins*. Bow at my greatness!

But enough bragging for now. Let's move on to the more mature love of third grade. The ~~victim~~ target of my affection was this totally cute and groovy boy. My two best friends thought he was cute n' groovy, too. In class, we'd swoon loudly in unison. When he walked by us our giggles rose to a crescendo. We'd pass him more love notes than he could count. How did that nine year-old boy handle it? With the skill of a politician.

Yep. The boy remained unflappable, treating us all with equal kindness. When our notes asked him which girl he liked the best he always answered the same way: "You're all great girls!" Thank goodness. If he had chosen one of us it would not have been nearly as much fun. I think he knew that, even if we didn't. Mutual crushes: the super glue that binds young girls.

Of course, a few of my crushes were a *tad* older than me. That's right. I liked older men -- much older, in fact, like Henry Winkler, also known as The Fonz. He was a character from *Happy Days,* a TV show that ran from 1974 to 1984. His slicked back hair and brown leather jacket? Irresistible.

I still remember penning a fan letter to him as part of a fifth grade writing assignment. I went on about how cute I thought he was and how much I loved his signature phrase, "Sit on it." In retrospect, it has to be one of the lamest tag lines in existence. Yep, the Fonz was dreamy. I fantasized about him all the time. Unfortunately, the same year I wrote the letter I found out the actor who played him, Henry Winkler, was 33 years old.

*33 YEARS OLD!* Holy moly! He was almost as old as my father! If I'd been older when I found out, the revelation would have led to a Lifetime Channel shower scene with me trying to wash the shame off. But I was ten, so I just took a bath and wrote "SAY NO TO OLD FARTS" in the bubbles with my finger. I couldn't believe that stupid Fonzie. Why did he have to be so cool, starting juke boxes with the pound of his fist? He was over three times my age! I knew I had to move on, and so I did. That is, until I hit another snag.

When I was twelve I had a major crush on a Monkee. No, not the cute, furry animal. I'm talking about one of The Monkees, a popular band from the late Sixties. Every afternoon I watched reruns of their show which featured Micky Dolenz, the funny one; Peter Tork, the shy one; Michael Nesmith, the one with the hat (don't ask); and Davy Jones, the totally hot and groovy one.

I LOVED DAVY.

He was soooo cute and, boy, could he rock the tambourine. I would spend hours daydreaming about him, envisioning us slow dancing to "I Wanna Be Free" in a flowery meadow while the sun's rays danced in our hair. So magical.

Well, guess what? A few months into our fake relationship I discovered Davy Jones was only 5'3". **5'3"!!** I was already 5'5" with no signs of shrinking and, as much as I loved him, visions of *his* head resting on *my* shoulder didn't have quite the same affect on me. I was devastated.

As I got older, and taller, my celebrity fantasies continued to suffer. Tom Cruise? 5'8". Johnny Depp? 5'10". Oh, the humanity! And not all of my celebrity crushes were ones to be proud of. The worst was Gopher from the *The Love Boat*. You heard me. I had a crush on a TV character named after a buck-toothed rodent. Don't judge me. He got me through many dateless Saturday nights in high school. Who needed a real boyfriend? Of course, the answer was I did. I was a teenaged girl. A boyfriend meant validation. A girl could be dull and dim-witted with a face that made kittens cry, but if she had a boyfriend she was cool.

I didn't date too seriously until my senior year of high school. Before then, it was more of a date here/dance there kind of thing. I hated it. One date did stand out, though, because during it I experienced TOTAL HUMILIATION.

**THE TALE OF DICKLESS DONALD**

This horror story took place during my sophomore year. Please note that Donald wasn't his real name. I've changed it to protect his innocence. Also note, he wasn't dickless -- at least I don't think he was. That kind of news spreads fast. In fact, Donald was not only good-looking, funny and sweet, he was two years older than me. Talk about a huge score! What he ever saw in me, I'll never know.

We had flirted with each other for months. One night he worked up the nerve to come over to my house. Unfortunately, that had been a big mistake because my parents were gone at the time. *But that's great*, you say. *A boy in your house without parents!* You don't understand. That meant my brother could roam about unguarded.

My stupid, smart-mouthed brother.

The evening started off okay. Donald had called beforehand, so I'd been able to prime my siblings. I asked my sister to kindly stay upstairs then told my brother, "Keep your bony butt away from us!"

By the time my date arrived, I had both siblings tucked away into their corners. My brother didn't stay in his.

So there we were, Donald and I, sitting on the family room couch engaged in awkward conversation. My brother, Jim, walks in, armed with a barbed tongue and a goofy grin. He looked at Donald and said, "Who are you?"

"I'm Donald," my brother's target replied.

"Donald?" Jim said. "With a 'd' as in 'dickless'?"

Donald just raised his eyebrows in surprise. Jim poked him with another verbal stick. "I hear you're on the golf team, Donald. Is that even a real high school sport? It sounds kind of pussy."

That's when I interrupted him with the sharp words of a mature older sister. "Knock it off, you stupid jerk!"

I shooed Jim from the scene. Still, the stage had been set for total humiliation. What? You thought the bit about my brother calling Donald dickless was the bad part? Oh, no. That was yet to come.

It was delivered by the hands -- no, make that *paws* -- of our sweet, silly dog, Buffy. No sooner had Jim left then Buffy entered the room, tail wagging with a smile in her eyes. She had something in her mouth. What the... It couldn't be.

Oh my God, it was.

Buffy had a maxi pad in her mouth. It wasn't a small one, either. It was HUGE! A ferret could have used it as a raft. I wanted to die. Immediately ripping it from her mouth, I stuffed it under the couch. Still, the damage had been done.

I was mortified. Donald was mortified. As for my brother? When he found out he was thrilled. Though Donald and I did go on a real date the next day, the mojo was no longer there. My attempt at a love life had been foiled by my idiot brother ...and Kotex.

*Buffy, the Romance Slayer*

### TO THIGH OWN SELF BE TRUE

But I did move on. Most of the guys I dated were nice. Not all of them, though. My first year of college I dated a real winner -- and by that, I mean he won the contest for being a jackass. Oh, those smoldering eyes, that sexy swagger, that untamed heart...

That *a-hole!*

Like in The Tale of Dickless Donald, I won't use this guy's real name. Why? Because people change. *He* changed. How do I know? Because he told me. But I'm jumping ahead. Let me begin at the beginning.

It was the start of second semester during my freshman year. Larry and I had met on a bus. We flirted, exchanging first names but nothing more. It took him a week, but he managed to track me down.

Impressive, right? He must have really thought I was special to go through all that trouble. Yep, I was all that and a bag of Cheetos. Larry made me feel that way for quite a while. He gave such great compliments. Then they became less frequent, but it was just us settling into the relationship. When a backhanded insult or two started slipping into the conversation it was okay, too. Larry only said them in the name of honesty. That was good in a relationship, right?

The descent was slow. It took awhile for me to realize what was happening. Then summer came and it all became crystal clear, thanks to the phone calls. Or lack of them. Larry didn't call me once, despite several messages from my end -- and I do mean *several*. I called three times over a span of six weeks. A phone stalker, I was not.

The last time I called I just said six words: "Call me if you love me." That got his attention. Larry called back the very same day, livid. What did I mean, "if he loved me"? Then he told me something which made me realize this guy was playing games. He said he was afraid if we talked this summer, I'd want to come and visit him. That meant I'd meet his parents and they would find out *he was dating someone with fat thighs*.

Let me back up here. The first thing you need to know is I was 5'10" and 120 pounds. I made a stick figure look like the Michelin Man. But I'd confessed to him one night that I'd always felt my thighs were just a little too big. (I know. A girl's self image can be so strange sometimes. Blame *Vogue* magazine.) At the time of my great confession, he'd just laughed. I couldn't be serious. Nothing about me was fat. I looked totally fine and that was that.

But that wasn't that, something I realized after he'd "confessed" about my fat thigh problem. Larry thought he could take my insecurity and use it as an emotional chip. He was wrong.

As soon as he said it I knew he was trying to mess with me. Did I call him on it? Absolutely. I kicked him to the curb like an empty Coke can. Actually, I just I told him to suck it then hung up the phone. He didn't call back.

That is, until late August. I had returned to school with nary a thought about my ex in my head. When I arrived classes had yet to begin so that night I went to a party and met a nice guy. Who knew? I thought. Maybe I'd see the guy again. Then Larry called my room at 12 AM. He sounded oh so sad. Poor thing. He begged for forgiveness, saying he'd been an idiot. Would I take him back?

Not on his life, I said, though I congratulated him on realizing he had been a moron. Still, he'd blown it. There was no going back -- not now or ever again. He should find another girl then treat her better than he'd treated me.

Larry didn't like that answer. He persisted. What did I do? I'm not proud. I lied. I told him I'd just spent the entire evening with a guy I'd just met. He was special and I was smitten. In fact, I said, I was pretty sure he'd be the guy I'd marry. Sure, I was just nineteen, but I could already tell this was going to be everlasting love.

Thank heavens Larry bought it. Though he continued to call, after a while that faded, too. I didn't see Larry again until our senior year. We locked eyes at a restaurant. He came over and said, "I really treated you badly, didn't I?" I agreed, "Yep. You sure did." He went on to tell me how he'd changed, how the experience had taught him an important lesson. "You were so brutal about it," he said. "Thank God. If you hadn't been, I might have never changed."

But he *had* changed. In fact, he had been seeing a great girl and things were going really well. Then he asked me about my dating situation. Was I still seeing that guy? I told him I was. The funny thing is, this time when I said it I wasn't lying at all. And you know what? Yep, you guessed it. In the end, I *did* end up marrying him.

So why do girls love bad boys so much? Is it the drama? The challenge? The whole "chasing after what you can't have" thing? I'm sure that's part of it. Plus all the books, TV shows and movies out there sure don't help. They keep telling us bad boys all have hearts of gold underneath those rock-hard exteriors. They're misunderstood. All they need is the right girl to transform them into angels. Who wouldn't want to be that girl?

Unfortunately, in real life 98% of bad boys are just, well, *bad*. It's not that they can't be fixed. They can. It's just that girls might not like the way it should be done.

If a girl isn't dating a bad boy, she should keep it that way and stay away from them. If she *is* dating a bad boy and the boy treats her like dirt, then she should dump him immediately.

Like I said, it's not a fun way to fix them but how else are bad boys expected to learn? By girls mooning over them and letting him treat girls like dirt? Not a good solution. Sure, girls could make up excuses in their heads, like, "he must be hurting inside" or "no one understands him," but do they really think that's going to help the situation? I'll tell you right now the answer is no. Showing them that treating a girl badly doesn't fly is the best thing that can be done. Trust me, if a bad boy wants a real relationship he will learn the lessons he is taught. The girl who teaches him those lessons may not get the final prize but, who knows? Maybe the sweet guy they do end up with will have been a former bad boy. That would be a happy ending.

As for my own happy ending, I must be honest. I didn't plan on finding my husband so soon in life. I wanted to graduate from college, set the business world on fire, *then* find the man of my dreams. But what could I do? I found him early. I could either marry the right guy at the wrong time *or* marry the wrong guy at the right time. In the end, I chose the right guy and I've never regretted it.

Please don't misunderstand me. We didn't marry right away. When we finally did I was twenty-three years old. That meant four years of dating -- two of them long distance. I became a pro at boyfriend maintenance.

Don't believe me? Then take a look at the wonderful tips I've compiled for girls. Trust me. You'll be bowled over by my wisdom.

### BOYFRIEND MAINTENANCE TIPS

First off, make sure to **tell your boyfriend you love him right away**. Sprinkling the word "marriage" into the conversation helps, too. Guys don't want to be kept guessing, plus they're hungry for deep, committed relationships. Starting out slow can end in disaster.

***Monopolize his time***. As you know, dating is a full-time job. There's no need for him to hang with his guy friends any more. This goes for you and your friends, too. Now, now. Don't worry. They'll all understand. Not only that, once your relationship is over they'll be eager to continue your friendship right where it left off. No hard feelings at all.

Okay, I realize there will be times when the two of you can't be together, sad as that is. When you're away from him it's important for you to **call or text him constantly**. Clingy is cool, plus all boyfriends crave a play-by-play of their girlfriend's activities. Remember: how many eyebrow hairs you've plucked + the number of blank pages left in your science notebook = fascinating!!!

Make sure to **use baby talk/kissy noises** whenever possible -- the more public the place the better. Boys love to hear it as well as participate, particularly when around their friends. Cute pet names, like Hugmuffin, Snookems, or anything ending in "poo" (Snugglepoo, Pookiepoo, Runnypoo- you get the idea) is best.

While we're on the topic of his friends, make sure to **tell them all of the sweet, romantic things your boyfriend does for you** when the two of you are alone. You may think the tips of his ears are red from embarrassment but, no, it's pride.

Never forget that dating is a competition. Therefore, it's important to **update your boyfriend on all of the nice things your friends' boyfriends are doing for them**, particularly if it involves money and/or gifts. If you don't, he might look like a loser. Then you'll look like a loser and…well, you know where I'm going with this.

Lastly, that whole business about just being yourself? As if! For your relationship to be a success, you must **pretend to like everything he likes**. So keep the channel on ESPN, cheer him on during *World of War Craft*. It may not be fun but you have a boyfriend and, in the end, that's all that matters.

Well there you have it – the extent of all my knowledge and wisdom. Yes, I know it makes having a boyfriend seem like a lot of work but, HELLO, it is. Your upgrade in social status makes it worth it. You might even make your friends jealous – bonus!

Okay, so maybe those tips were a wee bit sarcastic. I'm prone to do that now and again. What can I say? Sometimes you've got to have a sense of humor when it comes to the world of dating. When it comes to this next topic, though, I promise to be more serious. Why? Because it's about dating older guys.

## PINNED IN THE TAIL BY A DONKEY

When it comes to dating older guys I can't say I'm a fan. Not that I don't understand what girls go through. Boys their age can be so immature. If a girl wants a *real* relationship she needs to date an older guy, right? I mean, old guys are so much more sensitive, more understanding, more…I don't know. Grown up. Don't you think?

Well, if you really want to know what I think about that I can sum it all up in one word. Are you ready to hear it? Then here I go. Counting down from 3…2…1…

*Ewwwwww.*

First, let me set things straight. I'm not talking about teen girls seeing guys a year or two older than them. Three years older, though, and it starts to get questionable. A fourteen year-old dating a seventeen year-old doesn't fly in my book, but a nineteen year-old dating a twenty-two year-old? Not a felony. But once the gap widens to four years, I have to admit it gets creepy for me.

"But I'm wise beyond my years," the girl says. "I can handle a real relationship." This point I refuse to argue. In fact, for the purpose of this argument, let's assume she is wiser than the Great Horned Owl. Well, guess what? It doesn't matter. There's no way she's going have a real relationship dating a guy who's interested in a teen girl a lot younger than himself.

That's right. This has nothing to do with her. It has *everything* to do with *him*.

Sorry to break it to all the girls reading this, but a guy who dates younger girls isn't the cream of the crop. My guess is the girl would cringe if she met the same guy and they were the same age. On top of that, there's a really good chance something is seriously wrong with him – and I'm not talking "cute but troubled bad boy in math class" kind of wrong. I'm talking "life is a total dead end and I want to take you with me" kind of wrong. Either that or he thinks she's an easy target. Strike that. *Regardless* of whether there's something really wrong with him or not, he thinks she's an easy target.

As for the girl in this potential situation, I hope she doesn't think she'll look cool with a way older guy on her arm. Truth is, girls who date way older guys look: a) slutty, b) clueless or (more than likely) c) both at the same time. If her friends tell her otherwise, they're either a) lying, b) slutty, c) clueless…You get the idea.

So if you're a girl and an older guy comes up to you, acting all smooth and cool-like as they ask you out, just say, "Why don't you date someone your own age?" My guess is they'll either balk or counter with one of two stock phrases: "No girls my age are as hot as you," or "Girls my age are too complicated." Yeah, I'm sure they are. Truth is, they can't get a date with them -- either that or the whole easy target thing and, trust me, playing Pin the Tail on the Donkey might have been fun as a kid, but getting pinned in the tail by a donkey? Not so much.

Now with all that being said, I do understand there are some exceptions to the case. Still, I fear by just saying this every girl will think the exception applies to her case. The hard truth is guys who chase much younger girls are just plain trouble, or they're simply slow learners who threw away their boat tickets to Maturity Island. Either way, the odds aren't in the girl's favor, so why risk it?

My feeling is if you're the girl in question and your parents know the guy and think it's okay to date him, it probably is. I say *probably* because, let's face it, some parents are clueless. Others are downright scary, like if the guy slips them fifty bucks before he takes their daughter out on a date? I'm guessing that's a bad sign.

But that's another topic. Let's stick to the strange, confusing world of dating. It's not just hard for girls. In fact, there are times when I think guys might have it worse. Need a clue? Homecoming. Another? Prom. Yes, I'm talking about ohmygodIhavetoaskagirltothedance season.

### TWIST AND POUT

Did you know incidences of male stuttering increase 450% during the process of asking out a girl? That circumference of under-arm sweat circles goes up 600%? My guess is you didn't because those figures aren't true. Still, asking a girl out isn't easy, which is why I'm particularly disturbed by a certain trend I call The Big Ask.

Not all of you may know about this, as it may not have spread to all four corners of the world yet, but in good 'ole Iowa it's been going on for years. Guys don't simply ask a girl to a dance anymore. They go big, or stay home. Here are some examples:

White sporks strategically stuck into Kylie's lawn spelling out, "Will you go to Homecoming with me?"

------------------

The Burger King sign saying:
Hannah + Jacob
= Winter Ball?
Crispy Chicken Sandwich just $1.99

------------------

The bag of flaming dog poop placed carefully on Mallory's doorstep with the sign,
"Prom would be crappy without you."

Okay, so the last one wasn't very good, but you get the idea.

So tell me, who in the world dreamed up this humiliation? Isn't having the guts to go up to a girl and ask her out enough? What if she says no? It's one thing to have your ego crushed. It's another to know you spent $12.96 on four bags of Blow Pops so you could waste two hours mounting them on a poster board reading, "Life will suck if you don't go to the dance with me."

As a mother of a boy who will (hopefully not too soon) be entering the dating game, I must call for this madness to stop. If you don't agree, pretend you're the girl in this situation then answer me this: What if you don't want to go out with the guy who asks you? It's a lot easier saying no to someone who didn't just glass chalk the windows of your car with "The Top 10 Reasons U R Awesome." Another question: What if the guy just bags it? What if he decides he can't come up with something cool enough to do so he just decides not to ask you at all? It's been known to happen.

Okay, okay. So what if the girl already has a boyfriend. She knows he'll ask her to the dance and he knows that she'll say yes. Why not have a little fun? My answer to that is resource utilization. Save his energy for more important acts of subjugation, like taking you to see a chick flick or carrying shopping bags at the mall. Big Asks waste serious brownie points and with everyone trying to go green, girls should not be wasteful.

Let's face it. Girls are already high-maintenance. Stop the eye roll. You know it's true. So this time let's have the girl throw the guy a bone. Let's get rid of Big Asks.

I must confess, my original plea to stop this Big Ask business was back in 2011. Yet, as of this writing, there has been no change. I don't know. Maybe my persuasive skills need polishing. Regardless, it looks like I may need to come up with some cool ideas for my son when it's his turn to ask a girl one day.

Hmm…let's see.

He could egg his potential date's house, leaving a sign that says, "The yolk's on me if you say no to prom." Or he could fill a bag with decaying fruit, then put it in her locker with the note, "Homecoming without you would be rotten." I don't know. I'd better table this until my head is in the right place. Let's move on, shall we?

## ViOLeNT aCT of RaNDoMNeSS!
### THE GREAT EGG DEBACLE

    The time right after you break up with someone is rarely full of laughter and good cheer. Instead it usually involves some sort of sadness, rage, or unnaturally calm indifference. Well, one time a friend of mine back in high school took an unbridled path of rage. Or maybe it was just a path of pure silliness. I'll let you be the judge.

    She'd gotten all riled up about her ex-boyfriend and set her sights on revenge. The plan: egg the inside of his mailbox. I, of course, was totally against it. That's why you must believe me when I tell you that the only reason I came along was because I was forced. She and a few other friends had wrapped me in duct tape and shackled me to the back seat of her car. Honest.

    Anyway, late that night we drove up to his mailbox. My spurned friend armed herself with two eggs. Then, with wicked force, she let them fly from her hands. Man, what a SPLAT!

    Unfortunately, in her crazed excitement, she'd forgotten to roll her window down first. That big splat wasn't in his mailbox. It was all over the inside of her car. Strike that. It was all over the inside of her *mother's* car. Yikes. Still, it was such a hysterically stupid move, everyone -- including her -- burst out laughing. Then, abandoning the mission, we sped off in search of paper towels and Windex.

    Crimes of passion never end well.

## CHAPTER TWO
## People Be Crazy

Did you notice I had a whole chapter featuring boys, dating, celebrity crushes and I didn't mention *him*? Come on, you know who I'm talking about -- that bang flipping songster, Justin Bieber. It's been over three years and he's *still* on a lot of girls' minds. What's the deal? Of course, some of those minds are completely unhinged which is why I'm mentioning him here.

But before we jump into His Bieberness, I feel the need to make a general statement: People are crazy. They always have been and always will be. Allow me to offer some examples:

1. In the twelfth century, old mummies were abstracted from Egypt, ground to a powder and used medicinally. In fact, Francis I of France ate a pinch of it every day, believing it made him invulnerable to assassins. As late as the early 1900s, mummy powder was used to cure coughs, constipation, and other maladies. Crazy.

2. In Europe, from the thirteenth century until the eighteenth century, animals were put to a courtroom trial if they committed a crime. They went to court, had defense lawyers -- the whole nine yards. In one case in 1457, a sow and her piglets were tried for murdering a child. The sow was found guilty. Her piglets were acquitted. Crazy.

3. In 2010, during the Video Music Awards, Lady Gaga wore a meat dress. Crazy.

Craziness can be found everywhere, even in the most unlikely of places. Take the Bible. I have to admit, one of its stories really gets under my skin. Big time.

### "YOU'RE GONNA NEED A BIGGER BOAT."
I don't care if you're Christian, Muslim, Buddhist, or worship the ways of the Jedi, I know you've heard the tale of Noah's ark. God tells Noah about a huge, impending flood and instructs the man to

build a giant ark. Noah does what he is told. When the rain comes Noah is able to save his family as well as two of every animal. It's an age-old tale that's quite popular. Want to hear what drives me mad?

For years now, the Noah's ark theme has been a nursery room favorite. Tons of Noah's ark products are available for purchase -- crib bedding, lamps, pillows, pictures, to name a few. All feature cute little animals walking two-by-two into the ark. Adorable, right? Plus there are dozens of cute little books on the story, all aimed at the young and tender set. As for toys? Ay carumba! There are so many. Even Fisher-Price makes a Noah's ark play set. So what is my problem with all of this? Just the fact that NOAH'S ARK IS ONE OF THE MOST HORRIFIC STORIES IN THE BIBLE.

God condemns everyone. There's a huge flood. A fraction of life survives while everyone else DROWNS. *This* is the stuff bed time stories are made of? *This* is what we push onto our children?

For giggles I conspired with my friend and illustrator, TJ Lubrano. She's a wonderful artist with an uncanny ability to create sweet, whimsical pieces that make you want to smile. Much of her work would look beautiful on a child's bedroom wall. So I asked her to take the *true* tale of Noah's Ark and create a sweet, magical painting just for kids. I've got to say, I think she delivered. Tale a look below and I'm sure you'll agree:

Whoa! Who knew horror could be so cute? It's unsettling, all the same. What's with the world, turning this into a popular kids' tale? I can't figure it out.

But that's just the start. Look around and you'll easily find lunacy. Crazy people are not only everywhere now, they're armed with so many devices. They've got cameras, Facebook pages, and Twitter accounts. It's hard to escape them, which brings me back to super star heart throb Justin Bieber. What a lucky guy.

### YOU ARE WHAT YOU TWEET

Let's go back to January, 2011, when the Biebs finally found love. The lucky girl? Selena Gomez. She must have been over the glowing, white moon until psychotic Bieber fans started tweeting. Allow me to share some of the sweet congratulatory messages they sent Selena's way:

- *"I'll kill you I swear on GOD!!!"*
- *"If you are the Girlfriend of Justin I will Kill you I HATE YOU :@ !!!"*
- *"wh\*re cancer wh\*re...like i'm kill myself cuz I saw you and Justin kissing well thank you Selena thankyou now i'm killing myself"*
- *"stay away from Justin pedophile, retard wait i'm gonna kill ya in the night underneath your smelly bed"*

Ain't they sweet? I bet Justin would have dumped Selena in a heartbeat if he'd known he'd had chance with one of those pretty, pretty princesses.

Sure, there were other girls who told Selena "good for you" and "those girls are sick" but they don't concern me because they are sane. It's the haters I'm worried about. I think it's time someone gave them a good talking to. So if you fall into the sane category, just sit back and let these words wash over you. If you're one of the obsessed, however, listen up. The following is meant for YOU.

First of all, **knock it off.** You're acting like a moron. It's embarrassing. Not only do other girls think you're crazy, guys think you're REALLY crazy. Think they want to be with someone who goes ape crap over stuff like this? Kiss those potential dates goodbye. And by the way, while we're on the subject of dating, I hate to break it to you but **you've got no frickin' chance with the Biebs.** Not even one.

Now don't start arguing with me. I know all about the movie where the superstar singer drops his phone, a regular girl finds it then, after many touching and comedic moments, the two end as close friends. There's that other one, too, where the superstar singer accidentally hits a regular girl on the head, takes her to the hospital, blah, blah, blah, similar ending there, too. This "evidence" suggests it could happen to you, right?

Wrong. We're talking about movies, remember? As in *not real*?

You know, movies are a mixed blessing. They allow us to escape -- to believe the good guy always wins or gets the girl/boy in the end. Fantasizing about meeting the man -- or petite pop star -- of our dreams is kind of the same. It's like creating our own mini-movie in our minds. Most of us know life won't really play out that way. It's just a fun diversion. Others, however, need a wake-up call. So here is yours:

WAKE UP.

You're making a fool out of yourself, acting all mentally imbalanced and what not. Cut it out.

Seriously. I mean it.

Okay I'm done scolding now. I've got to tell you, crazy people drive me totally insane. And yes, I realize the paradox in that statement but I don't have it all together, remember? Still, one of the things I touched upon is a real sticking point with me. That's the fact that movies and television shows are so far-removed from reality. The whole bit about the superstar dropping his phone or knocking heads with you? That would be so cool. It would also be so Hollywood. Life just doesn't really roll that way.

## THE SECRET LIFE OF THE AMERICAN ACTOR POSING AS A TEENAGER

I have to admit I get kind of mad when a movie doesn't have a happy ending. It's a *movie*, which means it's *manufactured*. Why end on a bad note? I mean, come on. It happens enough in real life. Like I said, I go to movies to escape. Screw realistic integrity. Reality sucks. What kind of person charges moviegoers nine dollars to watch a guy sink to his watery grave while his new love remains behind, floating on a plank of wood? Sicko.

Thank goodness there aren't many movies and TV shows like that. Most stick to the Hollywood code. Sure, there's a lot more drama, but wrongs are righted. The good guy is rewarded in the end.

I'm curious. Would you rather live life like a character in a movie or TV show? For all I know, maybe you do. A while back, I decided to run with that question by delving into the serious, thought-provoking area of teenage TV dramas. I have to admit I was skeptical. Maybe it had something to do with my past addiction with the premier teen drama, *Beverly Hills, 90210*. No, not the wannabe knock-off but the original. You know, the one where the collective high school cast's average age was eighty-nine years old? Well, anyway, I didn't think anything could come closer to real teen situations and angst than that.

Oh, how wrong I was.

Take *Gossip Girl*. In 2010, its "teen" cast has a much younger average age of 24 years-old. Much more plausible. And the plot lines? Just look at the first season alone – teenage girls sabotaging fashion shows and kissing the wrong guys at masquerade balls. But of course. As for boys? We know they open up strip clubs ALL THE TIME.

Okay, okay. So those people are super-rich. Things like that *could* happen. Instead, let's look at a show that's more "of the people," like *The Secret Life of the American Teenager*. Those kids are more like it. Each and every one is obsessed with the only thing that matters in the real world: boinking. School, extra-curriculars, going out to the movies – as we know, things like that don't really matter. Just be careful, though. When you boink for the first time, your father will probably die in a plane crash. I mean it. Pregnancy, STDs, self-loathing or social humiliation? No problem, but HAVE SEX AND YOUR DAD WILL DIE.

Anyway, given this realistic change in programming, kids might wonder if *they* belong in a teenage drama. My answer is a definite maybe. With TV mirroring teen life so well, it's hard to tell. That is, until now.

Below is a scene that could take place at any lunch table across America. Kids can just follow along until they have a dialogue choice. If they find their typical conversations lean more toward choice #2 than #1, then they should start taking theater classes. After all, they'll be an adult before you know it and, thereby, able to play a teenager on TV.

Here it is:

***Tina***: Lori, you look so tired. You're not still (texting/conducting satanic rituals) with Sam all night?

***Kaylee***: No. I've had to start (working at Burger King/pole dancing) after school to pay for my (IPod song/doctor bills due to my secret fight club) addiction. It's wiping me out!

***Tina***: That sucks. But, hey, I've got an idea! Emily's mom is looking for someone to (mow their lawn/lie for them in a court case). Emily can't do it because she's (too busy with cross-country practice/flying to Paris for a fashion photo shoot). I hear the money's pretty good.

***Kaylee***: Jeez. Normally I'd say yes, but last week I went to Emily's and caught her parents (kissing/conducting animal experiments) in the kitchen. I'm too embarrassed to go back.

***Tina***: No way. Hey, isn't her dad (coaching her little brother's soccer team/a transvestite)?

***Kaylee***: He was until (John's dad took over/his parole officer found out).

***Tina***: What about Emily's older brother? He's only a high-school junior, but I hear he (already applied to two colleges/is dating our science teacher).

***Kaylee***: Seriously? I thought he (wants to go to State/is part of a high-tech smuggling ring). Hey, here comes Emily now. Let's ask. Just make sure not to say anything about (the huge pimple on her forehead/her evil twin's diabolical plan).

Now if you're an adult, it's a little easier to find out if you're prone to a drama-filled life. All you have to do is watch *Jerry Springer* or *The Maury Povich Show*. If you identify with any of the guests or the topics, you're in trouble. I suggest you bulk order DNA test kits now. Of course, if you're a mom and love flaunting your very special set of issues, I bet *The Real Housewives* is casting somewhere. Give them a call!

## GETTING TO THE ROOTS OF THE PROBLEM

Seriously, though, as far-fetched as some of the storylines are, you must admit they can be entertaining. And as far as crazy people go, they can be pretty entertaining, too. Enter reality TV! Jerry and Maury are just the tip of the iceberg. Why? I blame the intellectuals in our society. It's all their fault. They keep snubbing TV for more enlightening entertainment, like reading *The Brothers Karamazov* in

Russian to avoid contextual errors. What fun! That leaves idiots like us in front of the television screens, forcing ratings for TLC's *Here Comes Honey Boo Boo*'s ahead of The National Geographic Channel's... Well, let's just go with its entire line up.

Tell me, which would you rather see collide: two atoms or two raunchy fake-boobed bimbos chasing the same hot-but-total-loser of a guy? Don't answer that question. You might incriminate yourself and I'd like to do that for you a little later.

But before I do, I must explain how I feel personally corrupted by the Reality TV craze. You see, as a young girl, I was all about quality television programming. The evidence: my fascination with the much celebrated TV mini-series, *Roots*. Airing in 1977, this beautiful saga chronicled African-American author Alex Haley's family line from the enslavement of his African ancestor, Kunta Kinte -- the coolest character name *ever*, by the way -- to his descendants' liberation from slavery after the Civil War.

*Sorry, wrong poster*

It was pretty intellectual stuff for a ten year-old girl. Aren't you impressed? And to be clear, my fascination had *nothing* to do with one of the scenes where a recently captured African woman ran around topless on the deck of a slave ship as she was being chased by lecherous white men. Unfortunately, when that scene flashed on our television screen my parents sent me to bed. I was crushed. I'd never seen ~~boobs~~ action-filled drama like that before and desperately wanted to see more.

Despite my pleas to stay and watch, my parents told me I had to go. I was way too young. *Too young?* My age had reached double digits. I was totally mature! In fact, I'd just moved from liking plain old M&Ms to its more adult cousin, M&M Peanut. (Don't ask me how that made me more grown up. All I can say is I believed it to be true at the time.)

Storming up the steps to my room, I started crying when I hit the top of the stairs. From past experience, I knew the acoustics at that location was perfect. My sobs would carry perfectly.

But it was to no avail. Neither parent responded, probably because they were so enthralled with the show they said that I could no longer watch. So I went into my bed and continued crying. Still nothing. I had to up the stakes.

Then I came up with a perfect idea. I would fall out of bed! My parents would hear the dull thud of my body hitting the floor and rush right up the stairs. They would tell me they were sorry. It had been their fault. Had they let me stay up, this would not have happened. Then they'd let me go back downstairs to watch the rest of the show that night. It was a masterful plan, one I knew would work. I rolled off the bed, hitting the floor with a big thump.

It hurt -- much more than I had thought it would. Still, as they say, no pain no gain. Then I waited, masking my sly smile with a look of agony. I couldn't wait to see my parents' guilt-ridden faces.

Only they never came. Stupid *Roots*. Had it not been for the show, I know my parents would have come. But no. I guess they didn't want to miss another boob shot, even at the expense of their daughter's misery.

So there you have it. I've established my long running appreciation for fine television. That means I'm on a high enough horse to delve into the rest of the world's (certainly not mine!) fascination with today's TV programming.

Albert Einstein once said, *"Two things are infinite: the universe and stupidity, and I'm not sure about the former."* That may explain the situation I'm about to present. Take this girl. She's smart, beautiful, and talented. Her grades? Great, too, but only because she works hard to maintain them. She's on the volleyball team, is first chair in band, and just made National Honor Society, too. As for her boyfriend? He's a nice guy who treats her well. Her parents are pretty cool, as well. So, wanna watch a TV show on her life?

OF COURSE NOT. Her life's boring! But there's this other girl...

What a hot mess. Last year she quit school so she could work as a pole dancer to support her 10 month-old daughter. She's not sure who the father is, but no worries. Her sights are set on a new baby daddy. Will it be the heavy metal biker who likes to spank her in public, the stoner with a World of Warcraft addiction, or the totally hot ladies' man who also happens to be an assistant manager at the local pawn shop? Whoever it is, she better snag him soon -- her alcoholic mom is kicking her out of the house in a week.

YEAH, BABY! That's what I'm talking about. We wanna watch HER! And that, my dearies, it's what wrong with America today.

Okay, I get it. The drama is crazy fun and over-the-top characters are a scream. But I'm so tired of the media rewarding stupidity and bad behavior by giving morons TV shows. I mean, what does that say about us?

I know, I know. Just because you watch it, doesn't mean you'll act that way. I guess for most folks that is true. But there are others out there who aren't so bright. They take their cues from the media, like those girls who are trying to get pregnant so they can be on *Teen Mom* or the scores of people making embarrassing videos of themselves so they can be on *Real World*. Heck, some just do it for 15 minutes of fame on YouTube.

It seems we're moving from a culture that venerates the wise and honorable to one that idolizes the flamboyantly misguided. And while Snooki might have nabbed $150K per episode on *Jersey Shore*, there are a lot more wannabes out there spending their minimum wage paychecks on bronzer and hair spray hoping to make it big. Their chances don't look good.

Unfortunately, some teens HAVE found success this way, like those girls on MTV's *Teen Moms*. But *financial* success doesn't mean *personal* success. Just ask Amber Portwood. (If you really want to do that, send your letters to the prison where, as of this writing, she may still reside.) What's worse, for the girls to land the gig they had to do the unthinkable -- they had to become moms. I wouldn't wish that world of crazy on any teenager. It's hard enough doing it as an adult.

A while back, it was reported that some teen girls were so obsessed with fame they were trying to get pregnant in order to audition for *Teen Mom*. How delightful! Whether it's true or not, I don't know. The info came from nameless "industry insiders." Regardless, I feel the need to address any poor soul who, in the hopes of scoring fifteen minutes of fame, ends up with a million minutes of misery.

That's right. You heard me. MOTHERHOOD SUCKS.

## CHILLAXIN' IN THE TUB

Okay, so motherhood doesn't suck all the time, but I'd be lying if I said it's a bed of roses. Moms deal with a lot of crap, both literally and figuratively. Along with many great moments come a lot of awful ones…and boring ones…and bang-your-head-against-the-refrigerator ones, too.

Now before I continue, let me give props to *Teen Mom*. They don't glamorize motherhood and do a fair job of showing how hard it can be. Still, MTV is in the business of entertainment and what they highlight on the show reflects the most interesting parts of the girl's lives. "Interesting" doesn't always mean "good." In fact, a lot of it's bad. Still, it's interesting.

When you have a baby, there's not a lot of interesting. In the beginning, your life revolves around feeding the baby, rocking the baby, and changing the baby's diaper. Not the best prime-time TV fare. And those diapers? They don't smell like freshly baked apple pies and newborns go through at least eight a day. You have to feed them eight times a day, too, and not just during daylight hours. There are midnight feedings, 2 AM feedings, 4 AM feedings…. Get the picture? Trust me, when you have a baby you never look at a pillow the same way again.

As they get older you don't have to change their diapers and feed them as often. Instead, your time is spent running around after them making sure they don't ruin everything you own or, God forbid, get hurt. Until a kid is at least three years-old, if you don't watch them every minute they could die. Seriously. Did you know that most moms with young kids go to the bathroom with the door open? They're not exhibitionists. They just need to be available every single moment in case something terrible happens.

Don't believe me? One day I *really* had to (ahem) "go." Feeling brave, I left my then twenty month-old son on the couch and went to the bathroom fifteen feet away. I couldn't see him from there, but he was engrossed in *Dora the Explorer* so I thought I was safe. A few minutes later I heard a soft whooshing sound. Was water running somewhere?

Yep. As soon as I'd hit the john, my son had headed up the stairs and into the master bath's Jacuzzi. By the time I got up there, the tub was filled with five inches of water. He was too little to be able to get out of the tub on his own. If I hadn't arrived in time….Luckily, I arrived in time.

I'd like to say things like that didn't happen often, but I'd be lying. When you have a toddler, crazy stuff happens all the time. Their life is literally in your hands. As for that mention earlier about *Dora the Explorer?* Be warned. All those annoying children's programs, music, and toys will dominate your life. Forget *Pretty Little Liars*. You're on the *Yo Gabba Gabba* bandwagon now.

As kids get older things don't get easier. The challenges just change. There's so much activity! The next time someone asks for my address, I'm just going to give them my license plate number. Plus all the cooking, cleaning, and helping with homework. Holy frickin' moly.

Still, it's the mental aspect that's toughest for me. Even though I have good kids, sometimes we struggle to get along. Shocking, I know. Plus I love them with every fiber in my being and want them to grow into happy, successful adults. A lot of pressure goes with that. I'm constantly worrying about how well they do in school, if they have enough friends, if they have the right friends, etc. The worrying never stops. Heck, I'm in my forties and *my* mom still worries about *me*. When you sign up to be a mom, you sign up to place someone else's needs over your own for at least eighteen years. Is that worth a photo spread in *Okay* magazine? Not in my notebook.

Now I'm not telling people not to have kids. There's a lot of joy in parenting, too. I'm just saying they shouldn't have them when they're teens. There's so much life out there to be experienced beforehand. Experiencing it with a baby on your hip is so hard. Some things can't be done at all. Getting an education, travelling…even going out to a movie is tough. To give all that up for a shot at temporary stardom? Crazy.

I have a mom journal for each of my kids into which I write stories about them growing up. I looked through them yesterday. In the journal of my aforementioned son, "Jacuzzi" Paul, I found this little gem: "At age fourteen months, Paul actually opened up the oven and crawled inside. There's a first." Five pages later, I chronicled the day he read *Harold and the Purple Crayon* then drew murals on our walls with a purple permanent marker. So if you think I'm done with the whole "motherhood sucks" theme, you don't know me very well. In fact the next two chapters are devoted to that subject. Yep, it can really be that bad.

# ViOLeNT aCT of RaNDoMNeSS!

***Envelopes Have Sealed my Fate*** -- September 30, 2011

**NEWSFLASH:** I am going to hell and it's the United States Post Office's fault.

That's right I blame the mail. For years numerous organizations have been sending me heart-felt appeals for money and I've never given them a dime. Or should I say "returned" the dimes they so thoughtfully sent to me with the simple request that I return it along with a check for $10 -- $25 --- $100? How sweet of them to give me a choice. Still, I blew them off and pocketed the dime. My criminal behavior doesn't end there, either.

A group of unknown churches began sending me the most gloriously beautiful rosaries, crosses, and religious pendants you could buy from China for twenty-five cents or less. All they wanted in return was my cold hard cash. A noble request, indeed. I never sent them a penny. To my credit, I did hang onto the precious trinkets for a long time, though. Throwing away religiously inspired items, no matter how junky, automatically guarantees a first class ticket to Satan's after-life retreat, no? Recently, however, in a rage-filled junk drawer cleanout frenzy, I pitched them all in the garbage.

The devil made me do it.

Last week I sealed my fate. I stole from young children. The (name withheld to protect the guilty) School not only sent me exquisite foil flower stickers, two note pads, a 2012 calendar, and a frameable Certificate of Appreciation, but also included an actual dream catcher. That's right, one of those pleather-wrapped hoops with beads and feathers that are supposed to give people pleasant dreams.

*Exhibit A*

I have to admit, I was bowled over by their sweet, unsolicited and unwanted treasure trove of crap. And, to their credit, they understood that I might not want to send them money despite all of their hard work and expense. They wrote that, if I had to, I could just send them $5 to cover the expense of the gifts and call it a day.

I didn't.

See? I told you. I'm a cold-hearted person doomed to a terrible fate. Sure, I volunteer and donate money to charities I've heard of, but that can't make up for the countless number of free personalized address labels I have received over the years -- labels I've unscrupulously ripped from over-sized envelopes only to throw the accompanying solicitations away. I do promise you this, though. If you ever receive solicitations like the ones above, I won't judge you if you don't send them money. You can even use the stickers and notepads. But if you throw away a rosary, I can't help you. ;)

## CHAPTER THREE
## Motherhood Sucks, Part One - Let's Get Physical

You know the end of the last chapter when I said motherhood sucked so much it deserves two chapters? I exaggerated. Writers do that sometimes in an effort to heighten the drama. Sorry. I understand some of you don't believe me, surmising I "confessed" after one of my kids read what I wrote. But that's not true. My change in statement has nothing to do with the crushed look on their face as they asked me, "Is being my mom that bad?"

Of course it isn't. It's all sunshine and rainbows with just a hint of extreme horror mixed in. I just focus on the bad stuff so people feel better about themselves, believing their lives are better than mine. Also, I don't like to brag. If people want to hear about other kids' accomplishments, they can check their friends' posts on Facebook. People come to me when they want the dirt. Literally. I just direct them to the family room carpet.

Although, I am a good housekeeper. You can eat off my kitchen floor. Just scoop all the crumbs together and you've got quite a meal. As for that ring around the water line in all of the toilets? They're there on purpose to help the boys aim.

In all seriousness, the physical work that comes with being a mom really stinks. As I often do, I mean that literally. To compound matters, it never seems to end. That is especially true with the laundry.

### HAMPERED ATTEMPTS TO CATCH UP

A few years ago, we refinished our hardwood floors, making the kitchen and laundry room area off limits for a while. I didn't mind the kitchen part too much. It was kind of nice not having to cook. For dinner we just ordered carryout or had a pop tart tapas bar. But the laundry? It killed me. I had no washer or dryer for eleven days straight. To a mom, that's hitting below the belt. I just wasn't able to function.

Let me put it into perspective: Have you ever had your cell

phone taken away for eleven days? Well, it was nothing like that. It was worse. It was like living in a perpetual snow storm without a shovel. All you can do is watch helplessly as you get snowed in. Watching the laundry pile up feels the same, except that laundry doesn't melt. It just starts to smell funky.

You know the ancient Greek myth about Sisyphus, the evil king who was forced by the gods to continually roll a huge boulder up a steep hill, only to watch it roll back down right before he got to the top? That's laundry. On occasion, I go into a rebellious rage and wash every stinking sock and t-shirt in the house. Unfortunately, as soon as bedtime hits, the day's clothes come off and fill the empty hampers. Sigh.

Doing laundry is a task that has no end, like constant homework without a summer break. Only homework makes you smarter. Laundry turns your mind to mush. Maybe that's why I'm so weird.

**FOOD FOR NAUGHT**

In addition to laundry there are the meals. I don't know why but my kids keep expecting to be fed. They don't make it easy, either. As soon as I think I've got it all figured out, they throw me a curve ball.

Take the following example. It's such classic behavior I know every mom will commiserate. The product may be different, but the story is the same. It happens to all of us.

Here's how it goes…

The kids come home from school, all of them wanting a snack. One asks for Señorito Benito's Taquitos. I've never heard of them. "What?" he says. "I had some at a friend's house. They're fantastico! You need to buy some." So I do the next day. Finding them in the frozen food section at the grocery store, I get a box of twelve.

The next day, all three kids have Señorito Benito's Taquitos. It's a hit! They all love them. Finally, something all three will eat! Before I know it, we run out of taquitos. No problem, though. I buy another box. That one also runs out in a couple of days. What do I do? Buy more -- two boxes this time. That should keep the kids in stock for a while.

Nope.

Three days later the taquitos are gone. This is getting serious. I pull out the stops and do the only logical thing -- go to Sam's Club. There I find a super mega pack of 120 Señorito Benito's Taquitos.

Woo hoo! Not only do I have enough taquitos to last the kids for weeks, I get them for a great price.

Now every mom reading this knows what happens next. The taquitos don't get eaten. Why? Because as soon as you buy something in bulk it falls out of vogue. Immediately. From the time I left for the store to the time I got back home, all of the kids had moved on. They no longer eat Señorito Benito's Taquitos. In fact, the taquitos are officially crap. For a while I beg and plead my kids to eat them. Out of respect, they gag down one or two. But in the end, it's just me and a taquito-filled freezer, leaving me feeling like a chump.

And when it comes to food we're just talking snacks, people. Moms are tasked with providing kids three square meals a day. It's not easy for most. For others, it's a breeze. A few even like to show off their work. I admit, it bugs me a little. Why should they get all of the accolades?

A while back I decided to get in on the action. A Facebook status prompted me. One of my pleasantly perfect friends wrote a post (not even remotely) similar to this:

> Looks like I outdid myself again. The pork roast I made last night turned out great. I can't take credit for the baby carrots I grew in my garden, though. Thank Mother Nature for that! Blah, blah, blah...
>
> Like • Comment • Share • 8 hours ago via mobile
>
> 👍 2 people like this.
>
> Wow! I need the recipe. I was going to make filet mignon tonight, but that looks so good!
> 6 hours ago   Like
>
> I am such a loser...
> 5 hours ago   Like

That's right. She was fake flaunting her magnificent culinary skills, an area in which I'm sadly lacking. You see, as a mom, I have a terrible inferiority complex. I'm always worried I don't measure up. I don't want to be one of those women who bring home the bacon and fry it up in the pan. I want to bring home the bacon, fry it up in the pan, then crumble it into a savory Bolognese sauce and serve it over pasta al dente. Sadly, that isn't the case. Still, I try my best. So I decided to write a blog post featuring my culinary skills.

I featured the dinner I'd served that night. For my husband, I went all out and served him Banquet's Salisbury steak meal.

Ahhh. There's nothing like errant corn nibblets swimming in brown gravy to get the salivary glands going. Notice the potatoes, effortlessly stirred to make them extra fluffy. And that green stuff on the plate below the tray? A sprig of parsley, just like they do in fancy restaurants. Okay, so it's tarragon. I didn't have parsley. And yes, it's just dried leaves out of a McCormick's bottle. But I made the effort so I demand some credit. Would anyone else ever think to do that?

Don't answer that question. Instead, take a look at the beverage so beautifully positioned by the plate. I could have made lemonade from scratch, but that would have denied my husband his daily requirement of Yellow dye #5. Instead, I went with Kool-Aid lemonade made with an extra pinch of sugar because I'm sweet. Not only that, I served it up in a wine glass. Because I'm classy.

Since my kids rarely like the same thing that my husband and I do, I went a little crazy and microwaved something different for them: Banquet chicken pot pies.

Here's a sample. You may not be able to tell, but I went the extra mile and created a smiley face on the crust by poking holes on it with a fork. Yeah, that's me. Just adding a little extra magic to the experience. And, yes, after I microwaved it the face did look like it threw up a little bit, but I think my kids still appreciated the effort.

Scooby Doo fruit snacks were added as a side dish to fulfill their vitamin C requirement. As for veggies? No worries. Carrot cubes and peas were already in the pie -- so much nutrition in one place! Of course, I served up more Yellow Dye #5 in Olive Garden kiddie cups. Nothing like a touch of whimsy to make the dining experience special.

So there you have it: family dinner made special with a touch of Mom's love. Yep. I'm Miss Gourmet. Tell me, who's feeling inferior now?

### HELP ME, BRUCE WILLS

So when it comes to my kitchen, don't judge me and keep the heck out. Seriously, stay away. I know that sounds harsh but it's *my* kitchen. It is where I work. That means it's kind of like my office and I like my workspace clean. Notice I said I *liked* it that way, not that it was actually clean. Most of the time it's a pigsty. In fact, the only time my kitchen is spotless is when I have company. The illusion of a perfect life must be maintained. When people visit and say, "I bet it's this clean all the time," I chuckle politely and say, "I try." But inside I'm laughing manically, thinking, "The fools bought it! They actually think I'm a great housekeeper!"

Keeping the kitchen clean is a never-ending chore I just can't seem to master, though it's not totally my fault. Supernatural forces keep working against me. If you haven't seen the movie *The Sixth Sense* this revelation may confuse you. If you have seen it, however, you will know why I need Bruce Willis' help. Why?

BECAUSE ONE OF MY KIDS SEES DEAD PEOPLE.

How do I know? One day when I left the kitchen it looked like this:

When I returned a minute later it looked like this:

What. The. Frick. To my dismay, I still can't figure out which of my kids speaks with the dead. Could it be…

**kid #1**, who ate ice cream on the couch? (Which, by the way, is in clear violation of house rules.)

**kid #2**, who was sitting next to child #1 with a huge bowl of freshly made popcorn?

or **kid #3**, who was glued in front of the computer with a mountain of Slim Jim wrappers in his lap?

None of them would fess up.

In all seriousness, is it that hard to close a cabinet door? The task doesn't even require opposable thumbs. Even our cat could do it and, trust me, he's not that bright. He thinks the $2 teddy bear I bought for him at Target is his baby.

Unfortunately, I'm still waiting for Bruce Willis to show up so he can help me. I guess that means I'll have to solve this mystery on my own. After that I've got to take the kids' bathroom towels to the psychologist. They keep jumping off their racks and landing on the floor. Suicide? Really? There's has to be a better answer. The towels need help. I do, too. Where's Bruce Willis when you need him?

## THE SHIFT THAT KEEPS ON GIVING

It's not fair. When people say a mother's job never ends, they mean it, and it's not just the work, itself. It's also the knowledge that there's always something more that can be done *right now*. As I write this, I can *feel* the layer of dust on the bookshelves growing thicker, plus my shower door needs to be scrubbed. Like with the laundry, you're never finished. It's hard to take even one day off.

I still remember the day I tried to take time for myself. It was my first year blogging anniversary. I'd decided that day, as a treat, I'd just relax. I had my Lindt chocolate truffles in one hand, my favorite blankie in another, and a slew of *30 Rock* episodes waiting for me on Hulu. As for dinner that night, there would be no preparation. They'd all get mac n' cheese. Sure, I felt naughty, but deliciously so. I'd needed a break and knew I deserved one.

I'll have you know a lot of advanced planning and work went into ensuring I would get the stress-free "me" day I had so wanted. Unfortunately, the gods of misfortune and motherhood had been working against me. I received a letter informing me I'd never turned in some mandatory dental health form for one of my kids. A good portion of the day was spent downloading the form, running it over to the dentist's office, then sitting and waiting while it was filled out. Plus the folks over there scolded me because it had been eight months since my kids' last dental appointments when they should have been going every six months. As if I didn't feel like a bad enough mom for the whole didn't-turn-in-the-form thing. Now I was a mom who didn't care enough about her kids' well-being.

Plus, of course, the cat just had to throw up on the rug that day. Clean up took twenty-five minutes. So if you haven't already guessed, the Lindt truffles I'd reserved were gone in about half an hour. We're talking six truffles in a half-hour period. Still, I refused to calculate how many calories that equals because it was *my* day -- *MINE!* Unfortunately, I was the only one who seemed to understand this. Woe is me.

As I write this now, I realize there's an Ethiopian farmer on the other side of the world beating dry, dusty earth with a hoe with the hopes of growing something to feed his family. My life could be worse. Still, was one day too much to ask for? Sigh.

Okay, I'll quit my whining now and just pop another truffle in my mouth...Dang. Even *that* comment smacks of Marie Antoinette. I'd better stop and count my blessings. I'm pretty lucky and I know it.

## A SUPER POWER TRIP

Thinking about it, there are a few upsides to being a mom. It has helped me develop some awesome superpowers. So much so, I'm thinking about applying for membership with the Justice League of America. I don't think I will, though. The prospect of standing next to Wonder Woman has me a little rattled. There's not an inch of cellulite on her, plus her boobs are more buoyant than a helium-filled lifeboat. Still, there are things I can do that she can't. How do I know? Because I'm a mom. That whole "eyes in the back of my head" thing isn't a myth, and that's not all.

Without even having been there, I can tell when someone's taken a shower or sneaked a snack from the kitchen. When I sit on the couch, the arm chair covers don't come off -- I know! How do I do it? And last night, while I was sitting on that very same couch, I ate popcorn *and none of it landed on the cushions!*

*My Spidey senses are tingling.*

When I throw my clothes in the hamper, they make it in every time. At first I didn't think that was such a huge skill but my kids just can't seem to do it. As for my actual clothes, did you know I can take off my jeans without turning them into a pretzel? Not that it matters. Untangling clothes is another great skill of mine.

*Seriously, what IS this?*

I can also stop watching a YouTube video before it's even finished. I forced my sons to try that once. They actually writhed in agony! I must have a high pain threshold.

I won't even go into my ability to find shoes that mysteriously disappear in the closet, or my uncanny ability to hang a coat on a hanger. I don't want to gloat. As for getting stains out of carpets or someone's favorite shirt? Don't even mention it. I have a feeling, though, I might not be the only mom who can do all these things. Perhaps all of us are superheroes.

### AN UNUSUAL LIFE-SAVING DEVICE

Being a mom requires skill. Luckily for us, children start out small. They also start out stupid. Our number one job has nothing to do with chores. It's just keeping our kids alive. Think I'm being mean? Pishaw! There's a reason we kept the Drano under lock and key. Toddlers are particularly crazy -- a terrifying mixture of mobility and fearlessness. Remember that story about Paul and the Jacuzzi? That was one story out of way too many. He wasn't even our most reckless kid. That honor goes to Peter, Danger Boy.

When Peter was a youngster, I was confident he felt his mission in life was to make me stroke out at the playground. He was crazy. He'd run across the tops of monkey bars, climb on top of the roof topping the 20 foot-high twisty slide. How he survived, I'll never know. I don't know how I survived, either.

Luckily, one incident I did not see. That honor goes to my next-door neighbor. Peter had been climbing one of the trees in our backyard and, fearing he might fall, enlisted the use of our rope. About fifteen feet long, the rope was designed for swinging. Tied to a high branch of the tree, it had a large loop at the end of it to be used as a foot hold. Peter took that loop and put it around his neck. That's right, to protect himself in case he might fall, he put himself in a noose.

As for my daughter, Mary, she was an angel. I never had to worry about her doing stupid things. If she encountered a swing on the playground, she would swing. She knew slides were meant for sliding. On only one occasion can I remember her doing something even remotely dangerous. For a few weeks during the summer, right before she turned five, she took a shine to climbing on top of her Little Tikes log cabin. I constantly had to harangue her to come down. She would always oblige, only to climb it again. Of course, when her dad was present, she couldn't climb down herself. She always needed his help.

One evening, my husband, Rick, was outside in the backyard with her. She climbed on top of the cabin again. He told her to get down. Mary asked for help. Rick put his hands on his hips. "You got up there yourself and can get down yourself," he said firmly. She'd climbed up and down on her own many times. Mary whined, "Daddy, please," but Rick put his foot down. This climbing business had gotten old. So, once again, Mary climbed down from the cabin by herself, only this time she failed. In a flurry of arms and legs, she fell off of the cabin and broke her arm. Rick felt terrible. How fitting that Mary, our most sensible and careful child, was the one who ended up in the emergency room.

It's no secret that as a child's mobility increases, their parents' anxiety increases, too. You'll find spikes in fear when a kid learns to crawl, walk, ride a bike, and -- I don't even like to say it -- drive a car. When my oldest learned to drive, it was a cruel mix of physical and mental nervousness. Living in Iowa didn't help. Sit back, and let me tell you about it.

### DRIVING ME CRAZY

First, let me get this straight -- I love Iowa. The people are friendly and the corn is first rate. As I often say, it's a great place to live but I wouldn't want to visit here. As someone who grew up outside of Chicago, I don't miss the congestion and honking horns. Driving in Iowa is smooth sailing...until your kid hits fourteen years of age. You see, in Iowa that's when kids get their driver's permits. That's also when many parents have their first heart attacks.

Back in Illinois, I had to wait until I was fifteen for my permit. Then I took the mandated Driver's Ed course as part of my academic curriculum, learning to drive with the (insert high school sport here) coach at my side during the day and my trying-to-act-calm-but-ready-to-crap-in-his-pants father at night. After I completed the course and hit sixteen, I got my license. 'Nuff said.

From there I went through life foolishly thinking every place did things the same way. I didn't realize that in Washington, D.C. you couldn't get your full license until you were twenty one. (though now that I've driven there, I completely understand) or that Wyoming let's kids get their learner's permit at the ripe old age of 12 years and 9 months. And both places are so close alphabetically!

Lucky for me, my oldest wasn't hot to drive. When she hit fourteen, she didn't beg me for a permit. I didn't push the subject. When she hit fifteen, though, I thought she should really start practicing.

Agreeing, my daughter took the written test and got her driving permit. That summer, we enrolled her in Driver's Ed. (It's not part of the school curriculum here. That means high school coaches have to teach less important subjects like math and social studies, but I digress.) Before her class started, I had her drive around a little bit. You know, learn the basics. I didn't want her to start without any skills. Well...

I got a call from her instructor after her first time out on the road. It went a little like this:

*Instructor: Your daughter doesn't really know how to drive yet.*
*Me: I know. That's why she's in Driver's Ed, right?*
*Instructor: Um, that's not really how we do things in Iowa. Kids usually know how to drive before they take Driver's Ed.*
*Me: But you have those special cars with the double pedals/steering wheel combo. I don't. I'd kind of like to see my next birthday...*
*Instructor: I understand. Tell you what, from now on I'll take her out when there isn't any traffic. Have her meet me at the school at 6 AM, blah blah blah, blah blah blah blah.*

Sorry, once he said 6 AM I kind of tuned out. I'm happy to report, though, that she passed the course, although she will have to take a driver's test at the DMV before she gets her license. (Like she didn't have to before? What the what?)

Like I said, I love Iowa. It's a great place to live. I'm just too scared to drive around here anymore.

## HAVE YOURSELF A HARRIED LITTLE CHRISTMAS

Now before I end this chapter, I'd like to bring up one more stressful thing: the holidays. You know, those special times when moms try to make everyone happy and fail miserably? For many moms, including me, Christmas time is particularly stressful. Of course, not all of it sucks. There's still plenty of fun times and magic. It's just *we're* the ones creating it.

When I was young, getting ready for Christmas involved only two real tasks for me. The less enjoyable of the two was buying presents for my family. Better to give than to receive? Yeah, right. My gift selection was usually limited to the items at our school's Christmas Bazaar. It had the finest hand-crafted junk around. Anything made of felt, glitter or cotton ball snow could be found there, and at prices kids could afford. But that crap only met the standard for what I would give as a gift, not what I wanted to get. I had dreams -- *big* dreams -- which leads to my second task...

Compiling my Christmas wish list. No finer joy could be had. It was a job I spent many hours doing over many thought-filled weeks. No sugar plums danced in my head. I dreamt of Barbie Country Campers and Hippy Hops.

At the time, internet shopping wasn't even a twinkle in Santa's eye. We had no personal computers. We had to shop old school -- through catalogs, TV commercials, and the special section at Ace Hardware where they'd cleared shelves and stuffed them with toys. But the big thing was the catalogs. When the Sears Wish Book came out after Thanksgiving, I swore I heard the angels sing. It had dozens of pages in the back, all filled with wondrous toys. My siblings and I drooled over every page.

Anyway, outside of those two tasks there was little else I had to do. Sure, I had to make red and green construction paper mittens at school, but that goes without saying. As for the day before Christmas, there was only one major chore I was assigned to do. I had to polish the wood furniture in our house. When I finished, my fingers gleamed with Endust grease.

The day our company was set to arrive, my mom would always ask -- no *demand* -- that I do just one more thing: sit on my bed. Under no circumstances could I leave my room until the guests arrived. My sister and brother weren't allowed to move, either. My mom swore every time one of us came downstairs, we'd leave a wake of toys and grimy finger prints. I thought she was nuts. As a mom, I now realize she wasn't.

Let's flash forward now to the present. I'm a mom and it's Christmas time. OMG! There are so many cards to write, cookies to bake, and people to please. Let's not even get into gifts. I think one of the cards I made for the *Cards for Mom* portion of my website sums it up perfectly:

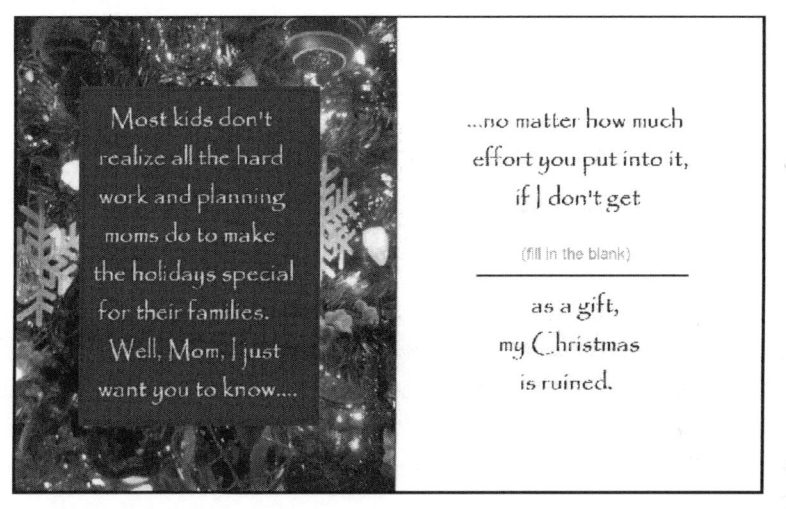

> Most kids don't realize all the hard work and planning moms do to make the holidays special for their families. Well, Mom, I just want you to know....
>
> ...no matter how much effort you put into it, if I don't get
>
> (fill in the blank)
> _____
>
> as a gift, my Christmas is ruined.

In addition to all the gift buying, present wrapping, etc. I have to keep the house spic and span, *and I don't even entertain*. The only family who comes to our house is my mother-in-law. And she's fabulous. I couldn't have asked for a more wonderful second mom. I love her dearly. But I just can't bring myself to let her discover that we live like barn animals most of the time. I have my pride.

Since we don't have Christmas at our house, it means we travel, which is a whole other ball of wax I'll discuss later. Just let it be said that Christmas time magic wears off a little when you're a mom and in charge of the whole thing.

Okay, I'm done now. Sorry if I've ruined a major holiday for you. In the next chapter, motherhood still sucks but in a different way. Read on to find out.

# ViOLeNT aCT of RaNDoMNeSS!

### *Dear Make-Believe Mom* -- *April 29, 2010*

**Dear Mom,**
It's hard to explain. I mean, I don't go out a ton, but I do have friends. Still, sometimes I just feel so alone, like I don't fit in. What should I do? - **The Only Lonely**

**Dear Lonely,**
Rejoice! Yes, you heard me. Why? Because it means you're normal. If you didn't feel that way you'd be a freak. Seriously. No one feels 100% comfortable with themselves 100% of the time. Okay, I know what you're thinking: What about that girl in math class, the one with the coolest clothes, coolest friends, etc.? She never feels that way, right? Wrong. Just don't ask her to admit it unless you want her to give you the stink eye. Even still, what if she *did* think she was all that 24 hours of every day? Talk about a major head case. Nope, I'd rather be you. People who know what it's like to feel awkward are usually nicer and make better friends. My bet is you're one cool, compassionate chick.

**Dear Mom,**
I've been dating this guy for a while now, and he's been pressuring me to play Monopoly. Thing is, I'm not sure I'm ready. What should I do? - Not Quite Ready to Play

**Dear Not Quite Ready,**
Wow, Monopoly. I can see why you're scared. The game takes so long to set up, yet you have no guarantee your boyfriend will keep playing after just a few turns. If he does keep going, it can be hard to tell if the only reason he's doing it is so he can hit GO and collect

$200 all the time. Then, by the time you figure that out you've got so much invested in the game you feel you have to keep playing even when you want to stop. ARGH! The social repercussions can be devastating, too. All it takes is for one person to find out and, before you know it, the whole world is snickering about your Community Chest. Tragic. Plus, there's always Chance. Pick the wrong card and the game's over, just like that. Talk about a messy clean up –- there are so many pieces! -- and, more than likely, your boyfriend won't lift a finger to help.

My advice? Don't roll the dice. Stick to simpler games until you want, and can afford, to buy Boardwalk and put a house on it. Trust me. Your life will be happier and much more care-free.


**Dear Mom,**
I'm sixteen years old and wear a size 11 shoe. I feel like a circus clown. Any suggestions on how I can blend? - Bigfoot in Smallsville

**Dear Bigfoot,**
Now I've been pretty straight forward with advice so far, so I know you're expecting something like, "Size 11 shoe? No big deal. I bet no one really notices," or "Accentuate the positive! I bet you can clog dance louder and squash bugs better than anyone else around!" Truth is, I'm sure you look like a total freak and, as a teenager, the last thing you want to do is stand out. Conformity is king so the solution is simple: remove your toes with a hacksaw. I know it sounds painful, but not as painful as the total humiliation you must be going through. I mean, I still remember the day I had to break off my friendship with a good buddy once I noticed her knees looked a little too much like russet potatoes. Sure, you'll have trouble walking and wearing flip flops will be a thing of the past, but now you'll be able to really rock a pair of Uggs. Totally worth it. Just ask your parents first. Doctor bills and physical therapy will play heavily in your future.

# CHAPTER 4
# Motherhood Sucks, Part Two - Emotion Sickness

Now as I intimated from the end of the last chapter, the strains of motherhood are more than just physical. In fact, many will tell you the hardest part of being a mom is the mental/emotional stuff. I agree. Kids will stomp on your heart, flatten it out with a rolling pin, then turn it into a bow tie to wear around their necks. The worst part is they don't even realize they're hurting you. It's just part of their modus operandi.

The day when a kid finally decides they're too old to kiss their mom goodbye in front of their friends? A stab to the soul. And when they present their mom with a box of all their stuffed animals -- including the teddy bear they used to sleep with every night as a toddler -- and said say they don't need them anymore? Heartbreak Hotel. And when they're in the mall with their mom and keep walking twenty steps ahead so people think they're alone? No one is fooled. Their mom isn't either. The only solace is that their mom probably did the same thing to *her* mom while growing up.

But it's not just about watching your kids grow up. There's a whole lot more heart break and worry to go around. Every mom has their own stories to tell, including me. Let me tell you one of my worst.

**THANKS A LOT, PAJAMA SAM!**

Little Petey was not quite four years old at the time -- too small to be out in the world all alone. Unfortunately, he didn't think so. Peter was an explorer! He had things he had to do, people he had to see! You know those sliding chain locks they have on hotel room doors? We had to install them on all of our exterior doors when he was only two! The boy had to be contained. I knew it. My husband knew it. Our parents and friends all knew it.

Our babysitter didn't.

It was a very hot summer day, pushing over 90 degrees (a fact that will be important later). A friend was in town and we'd decided to go out for just an hour or two. Her daughter had said she'd be happy to babysit. She'd done it for me before. So we left her at home with Peter and my daughter, Mary.

Devious Mary.

First let me set things straight. Mary was and is a totally awesome kid. She always did what she was told and rarely got into trouble. I take no credit. She was just born that way. She did, however, like to do one terrible thing. She liked to mess with her little brother. What kind of kid does that? Every kind. I swear it's in children's DNA.

Mary knew Peter was fearless. Nothing in this world terrified him, save one thing. *Pajama Sam*, a computer game she liked to play. It was like kryptonite to him. Every time she popped the game disc into the computer and hit "play" Peter would run from the room, a horror-filled scream on his lips. Because of this, we'd rarely let Mary play the game, something she didn't like at all.

Anyway, after a couple fun-filled hours, my friend and I returned to my house. We entered the kitchen. Sitting at the computer were Mary and the babysitter. They were playing *Pajama Sam*. I immediately scolded Mary, "You know you shouldn't be playing that." With a secret smile she said, "I forgot." Then I asked where Peter was. The babysitter said he was upstairs so I went up to find him.

Peter wasn't there.

I looked everywhere, starting with the top floor, then the main floor until I finally hit the basement. No Peter. I went through the house again. Then a third time. It wasn't just me. Everyone else was looking, too. We couldn't find him. I started going through the house for the fourth time, starting with the drawers to my bathroom vanity. The drawers couldn't have measured more than 6 inches wide or deep -- too small for a loaf of bread, much less a child.

I had to force myself to stop. Peter was not in the house. Reality set in. I ran out of the house into scorching heat and screamed his name.

Nothing.

We searched for him. He had either run away or he was hiding somewhere small -- perhaps a place that was hot, where he could suffocate if he stayed too long. I ran back into the house.

Then I called the police. It was surreal. I don't even remember what I said over the phone. The whole world started looking so blue, fuzzy. My body felt so cold. I couldn't breathe. When it sunk in there was a good chance I'd never see my son again, the knot in my chest tightened further.

I started running around the neighborhood while my friend stayed back to wait for the police. She didn't tell me until later that when they came they had ransacked the home in desperate search for Peter. Bless her heart. She cleaned everything up before I got home, which was twenty minutes later. Then it dawned on me: I had to call Rick and tell him that Peter, our son, was missing.

Thank God the phone rang right then. It was the police. They'd found Peter two and a half blocks away. He had walked into a cul-de-sac and, not knowing how to get out, had sat under a shady tree. Luckily, the man who owned the house where that tree stood had come home and found him sitting there. Why had the man gone home in the middle of the day? A phone call he'd received at work. His dog had run away from home. Yet another escape artist.

The man told me later that when he came home he was a little surprised to find a boy under his tree. Walking over to the boy, he'd said, "Hey, buddy. What's going on?"

Peter had replied. "My name is Peter from Iowa and I am lost."

Then the man had said, "Let's try and find your mom."

"I can't go home," Peter had replied. "I'm in BIG trouble."

Luckily, a girlfriend of mine lived a few houses away from the gentleman's home. Luckier still, her husband was home. As he was sitting in his study, he looked out the window and saw what was going on. Spotting my son, he beckoned my friend to the window and asked if she knew the little runaway boy.

She did, so when my friend and husband saw a policeman driving around our neighborhood, they knew to flag him down. A few minutes later, I got the policeman's call saying he'd found Peter. He also said Peter refused to get into his car to go home. He'd only go home with Mom. "Getting into a stranger's car is dangerous," he'd told him.

Little Petey: poster child for safety.

When I arrived at the scene I could tell Peter felt like a rock star with all those people around him. He had such a big smile on his face when I ran up to him and gave him the biggest of hugs. I thanked everyone -- the cops, the neighbors, the saint for misguided children -- then told Peter it was time to go home. His warm demeanor turned cold. Taking a step back from me, he asked, "Are they still playing *Pajama Sam*?"

Now that I got that out of my system, let's move on to my second heart-pounding tale. This one also involves Peter, not because he's a bad kid but because he is such a great sport. You know the classic teen nightmare where the mom shows naked baby pictures to a kid's boyfriend or girlfriend? If I ever did that to Peter, he'd probably laugh and say, "I look hilarious!" Which is awesome. Sure, it reduces my options for blackmail but I'm glad he has a good sense of self. Though, mind you, having a good sense of self is different than having sense. Allow me to explain...

**UNCOMMON SENSE**
After Peter ran away we did our best to drill one important thing into his head: he could not leave anyplace without us -- not our house, grandma's house, the grocery store, library, school, etc. By the time he was close to nine we had the whole "don't leave without us" thing under control. At least we thought we did. My bubble burst during the summer of 2007.

The day had started out well. I had mastered an unbelievable feat as a mom. I'd gotten all three kids signed up to take swimming lessons at the very same time and place. Not only was that logistically awesome, it also meant I'd have some free time all to myself. Thirty-five minutes. I said, *thirty-five glorious minutes!* That's 185 minutes in harried mom time, or maybe that's dog years? I don't know.

Anyway, it was an outdoor pool so I could watch my children during their lessons. Each kid was in a different group so, on the first day, I stuck around just to make sure everything went well. It did, making me confident I could leave. Big mistake.

The next lesson day I decided to take a walk. Me doing something by myself! It was just too good to be true, I thought to myself. I was right.

Though I had thirty-five minutes, I came back after just fifteen. Why push the envelope? Scanning the pool, I searched for my kids. Mary? Check. Paul? Check. Peter?

Peter?

He was gone. It was five years ago all over again. Where could he be? I rushed into the pool area. Nothing. Into the locker room. Also nothing. Going back to where the lessons were held, I ran up to Peter's teacher and asked where he'd gone. "I don't know," she said. How encouraging. So nice to know *no one* had been keeping an eye on my son.

Though I wanted to beat her over the head with one of those floaty noodles, I refrained. My subsequent arrest might keep me from finding my son and I *had* to find my son. Luckily, I found him a few minutes later hanging out in our car. I was livid. As soon as I opened the car door I yelled, "What are you doing in here?"

"Just taking a break, Mom," he said nonchalantly. "I didn't want to be in lessons any more."

"So you just walked out? Peter, we've gone over this so many times. Never leave anywhere without me or Dad!"

"You never said that," he replied. "You said I couldn't leave our house, or Grandma's house, or the library, or the store, or my school. But you never said anything about leaving the aquatic center."

He had me there.

I shook my head. "Peter, you need to learn how to generalize when I explain things to you. When I said not to leave those places, I meant you shouldn't leave *anywhere* without me."

"Oh," he said, looking truly surprised by my sudden revelation. He thought on it a minute then said, "Mom, I just realized my fatal flaw."

"Your *fatal flaw*?"

"I have no common sense."

Man, the boy sure hit the nail right on the head. Smart kid, that Peter.

So when people say being a mother is an emotional rollercoaster, they are serious. Thank goodness there are a few laughs along the way, as well. Otherwise, I'm sure I'd lose my mind. Even so, the job can be thankless. It's amazing how much I put into being a mother. More amazing is how little I get in return. If my kids were mutual funds, I'd have kicked them to the curb alongside my no longer prized Beanie Baby collection.

Sorry. I know I sound harsh but sometimes I feel so under appreciated. Like the time I got the game *Boggle*. My kids let me down. Big time.

### BORED GAMES

Growing up, I had loved the game *Boggle*. My family played it all the time. So when I got it one Christmas I was thrilled, hoping to re-create some old-time family fun magic. I asked kid #1, if she would play it with me. She responded with a roll of her eyes. Kids

#2 and #3? Same thing. NOT ONE KID WOULD SACRIFICE THEIR PRECIOUS TIME TO PLAY A GAME WITH THEIR MOM.

Yeah, yeah. It may sound petty to you, but you've got to think about where I was coming from. In the last decade and a half, I've done my part in being a good sport. Here are some examples:

- I've played *Candyland* and *Chutes and Ladders* over 3,267,014 times. Oh, the joy I felt of witnessing crushing disappointment when a child landed on squares forcing them back near the beginning of the game. The fact that it extended game play an additional half hour was even more pleasurable.

- In the hours upon hours of Barbie play time I've played the roles of Ken, Barbie's sister, Barbie's mother, Barbie's teacher, Barbie's cult leader, but NEVER BARBIE. Always a bridesmaid, never a bride.

- *Elefun*? More like *Elepain-in-the-a\*\**.

- Devoting five full minutes to set up *Don't Break the Ice* only to have some sweet toddler with a demonic facial expression smash the whole dang thing in two seconds flat? MOST. FUN. EVER.

- The game *Sorry*? I totally was.

- Do you think I ever got to choose my game piece color first? Nope. I always chose last. Getting the race car in *Monopoly* was a dream never realized. It still haunts me.

I could go on, but it's just too painful. Yet I did it all with a smile folks, even when I was pleading inside for sweet Jeezus to take me away. And where is my reward? Certainly not sitting across the table from me, pencil and paper in hand, ready to find as many words as possible in three minutes flat.

That's right. You heard me. ***Boggle* takes only three stinkin' minutes to play.** Oh, how it feels to be appreciated after all those years of torture. Thanks, guys. Thanks a lot.

I swear, sometimes I feel like Rodney Dangerfield in full make up and a dress, getting "no respect." (Oh, man. A mental image of Rodney Dangerfield in that makeup/dress combo formed in my mind. Did that happen to you? If so, I'm sorry. If it hasn't, because you're too young to know who Rodney Dangerfield is, I suggest you watch the movie *Caddyshack*. STAT.)

There are also times when kids are just big whiny pains in the arses, adding to a mom's misery. It's not like they're bad -- though sometimes they are. It's just that they are kids. At times it feels like the only thing worse than having one kid is having two of them. Or in my case, three. There is something about siblings. Boy, can they get under each others' skins. You know, I think new energy research should be directed toward the tension that can occur between two kids from the same family. I swear, there's some element in siblings' systems that, when combined, turns absolutely nuclear.

I remember a little piece I wrote one year in anticipation of Mother's Day. What did I want for a gift? Flowers? Chocolates? Jewelry? Nope. Not even close. I'd wanted something much more precious -- and much more elusive -- than any of that.

### CHANNELING GRETA GARBO

Now before I tell you what it is, please note I've received some interesting Mother's Day gifts over the years. There was the dyed macaroni necklace (always a classic) and dinner out at my "favorite" restaurant, Chuck E. Cheese. There was the marigold nestled in a hand-painted pot that had been kept "safely" in a sealed paper bag for five days. Poor plant. And I loved them all. What can I say? I am a mom which, therefore, makes me a freak.

Anyway, as my kids have grown older, my gifts have grown up, too. Case in point: my favorite restaurant is no longer Chuck E. Cheese. It's Steak and Shake. I'll wear my pearls the next time we go. The kids have learned that as beautiful and valuable as gold glitter is, they shouldn't put some in an envelope and give it as a gift. They've also learned that, if they *do* give me glitter and it lands all over the carpet, Mommy will cuss.

Okay, let's end the suspense. Want to know what I wanted for Mother's Day --what I've *always* wanted each year? Here's a clue: my teen daughter knows what it is? Why? Because every day she wants the same thing.

ON MOTHER'S DAY I WANT TO BE LEFT ALONE.

Okay, I know that sounds un-mom-like. Mothers love their kids. They want to be with them all the time, right? Well...

It's not that I don't have good kids. I do. It's just that they, well, *they act like kids*. Okay, I'm digging myself into a hole here so I'd better explain. Here's what I really want:

- **No groaning.** When I ask someone to take out the garbage I want to hear, "No problem." I'll consider words like, "You work so hard, it's the least I can do," as a bonus.

- **No complaining**. If someone's tired of eating spaghetti again, today I'd like them to keep it to themselves. If going to Aunt Zelda's "totally ruins" their weekend, they can tell it to the posters in their rooms, not me.

- **No fighting**. If one sibling enters another sibling's room without asking, just this once I'd like the sorely afflicted victim to refrain from chucking a Darth Vader bobble-head at the perpetrator's left temple. Is that so hard?

- **No mess**. Simply said, just pick it up. I'm tired of nagging on the subject. For one day I just want it done.

In other words, I just want peace. No need to add "and quiet." JUST GIVE ME PEACE. Is that so hard? If my kids want to throw in a Vera Bradley bag or a Dr. Who floating TARDIS that would be nice but, dang, please add peace to the equation. I'm just asking for one day of the year, after all. They've got 364 days left to drive me crazy.

## SAY YES TO THE STRESS

Of course, the strain of parenting doesn't just come from the kids. I put plenty of pressure on myself. It seems these days your identity is tied more to your kids than anything you do on your own. And that's not fair -- not just to the parent but the children, too. It stresses out *all* of us.

Take summer time. Back in the day, summers meant playing kick the can or working on a tan in your back yard. These days, once school is officially out my life gets officially crazy. Sure, I can sleep in a little more and the burden of hounding the kids about homework has stopped, but those things don't support my argument so, instead, I'm going to focus on all the extra meal-making and chauffeuring I have to do.

To make it easier on me, I did try to get a new car for my daughter, but the dealership refused the trade. (Insert rim shot here.) Seriously, though, I'd like to talk about the hardest thing there is about summer: the pressure to make sure my kids are "productive."

These days summers seem to be less about relaxation and more about getting ahead. It's weird. We've got a lot of kids in our neighborhood but I rarely see them around. They're all at camps, classes, and practices to increase their skills -- to make them stronger, smarter, better. I'm curious, am I the only one who thinks this is strange? When did the bar get set so high? When did pick up baseball games at the local park turn into daily practice and weekend tournaments three hours away? Kids are taking ACTs when they're sophomores, or younger. Private tutoring is a booming business. Plus it seems like a parent's social status revolves more around their kids' accomplishments than their own. That's a lot of pressure -- for both parents and kids - -causing headaches all around. Plus we all know the higher we raise our expectations, the greater our chances for disappointment.

I know, I know. Global competition is fierce. The economic gap is widening. A lot of parents are worried that their kids won't grow up to have lives as good as what they've got right now. Parents want to give their kids a fighting chance, but are they giving them ulcers, too? And this "program for success" we're feeding them, does it allow their independence and creativity to blossom?

I wish I knew the answers to all of this, but I don't. I just know that I don't like it. But if I boycott this movement toward over-parenting, will that put my kids at a disadvantage? Kids today seem smarter and more talented than they've ever been before. Still, statistically, half of them are below average. Scary thought, huh?

When it comes to the stress of parenting there are issues that run even deeper than a kid's achievement -- issues that are out of a parent's control, which makes it all the more challenging.

**QUEER FEARS**

I love my kids -- not just for what they do but for who they are. Sometimes other people don't share my feelings. It's not always easy being yourself, particularly when you're a teen. How I wish I could protect my kids from the big, bad world. It's hard knowing I can't. Which brings me to my next subject. I'll be honest, it's a topic I almost chose not to cover in my blog a couple years ago. Why?

Because there are people out there -- some that I know -- who, frankly, don't agree with me. It's a polarizing issue, a fact that saddens me. I may have lost a reader or two. But this was an issue I felt too strongly about to ignore. (Spoiler alert: It's not about low-slung jeans and butt cracks. That one comes a little later.)

A while back a fellow blogger mom rocked the internet with one of her posts. She wrote about how her pre-school son wanted to be Daphne from *Scooby Doo* for Halloween. The boy loved the cartoon show so she let him. No big deal, right?

Wrong. To a few other moms it *was* a big deal. How could she allow her son to dress up like a girl? People might think he's gay. My God! He might even *be* gay. Oh, the humanity! The woman ended up sticking to her guns and told the other moms to back off. For that I applaud her. As for calling those moms out in front of the entire world? I don't know. I doubt it made her son's life easier.

Anyway, it made me think -- and write -- about how I would feel if I found out one of my kids was gay. How would life be different for them? How would they fare? I'd be lying if I said I'm not a little worried about the issue. Not that I care whether or not one of them is gay. They are who they are and I'll love them regardless. Plus there are a lot of super cool gay folks out there. Just watch TV. There's Ellen DeGeneres (funny), Jane Lynch (funnier), and Squidward (hilarious), as well as knowledgeable experts like Anderson Cooper (news), Suze Orman (finance), and Tim Gunn (making it work). It's just that being gay can be so, well, *hard*.

I know that for most it gets easier after teendom, but when I look at all the stories on the news lately -- the bullying, the suicides -- it breaks my heart. I can't imagine the pain and torture those kids went through, the pain other kids are going through right now. When I was a teen, I felt so lonely at times. No one understood me. I struggled to fit in. If you saw me walking down the halls you'd have never guessed I felt that way. I kept it all inside. Isn't that what you're supposed to do, keep it inside?

And I was "normal." I can only imagine how hard it would be to go around worried that people might discover who I am and not like it, to live in a society rife with messages saying how I felt inside was wrong. I worry about how difficult it would be knowing that there were people in the world ready to ostracize or hurt me simply because I was different.

It's hard to admit this, but I don't want that for my children.

Having straight kids would sure protect them and me from a whole lot of pain. I know our society has come a long way in its acceptance and understanding of others, but it has such a long way to go. It scares me. My love alone cannot protect my children. I want them to be happy. I want them to be safe.

But I want them to be themselves, too. Being gay isn't a problem. Living in a world that doesn't fully accept gay people is.

So let me make an open statement to my kids right now: *If you're gay, don't feel you have to hide it from me. I love you just the way you are. If other people don't like you because of it, screw 'em. They're missing out on one great kid, plus there are plenty of folks out there who could care less how you slice your sandwich. Hang in there, stay strong, and know I'll always be your soft place to land.... Now go take out the garbage. You heard me. Just because you're gay doesn't mean you don't have chores. Sheesh!*

Okay, I'm done with the "very special episode" part of this chapter and ready to return to our regularly scheduled silliness. Only this time, it isn't me playing the role of the stressed parent. That honor goes to my mom. From what I gather, she had more than a few rough moments of her own. I know I starred in a few of those tales. In fact, I'll prove it. Here's one of them now:

## LOVE, MARRIAGE, AND FRUIT CUPS

Before I start, let me announce that Rick and I have been married twenty-two years and counting. Huzzah! It's been a wonderful, crazy ride and there's no way I'd give any of those years back. As for planning the wedding, though? I could have skipped it. Thank goodness for my mom. I leaned on her a lot. You see, my life was so crazy at the time. I had just graduated college and was looking for a job. All my mom had to worry about was her job, house, husband, two kids in college, one back at home (me) and a dog. Plus she wanted the wedding to be perfect and, with her help, I knew it would be.

She went everywhere with me -- dress shops, florists, photographers studios, reception halls. We made every decision together, except one: the menu for the wedding reception. Mom was busy the night we had to choose the food selections, so my dad and I went alone. (Side note: If you're wondering where Rick was during all this, he was one hour away finishing school. He had no time to breathe, let alone help. Poor, lucky thing.)

Anyway, the night was fun. Dad and I chose French onion soup to start. For the main course we selected prime rib, a baked potato, as well as salad on the side. We chose the cake, too -- black forest, my favorite. The whole meal sounded absolutely yum! When Dad and I finished, we patted each other on the back. Job well done!

Then we came home and announced the menu to Mom. She smiled at us sweetly. "Are you sure about starting with French onion soup? It can be salty. It might ruin people's palates." Dad and I assured her that everything would be fine, plus the alternative to that was a fruit cup. We all knew how fast bananas browned. The fruit cup could end up pretty nasty.

And that was that, or so I thought as life continued on. I found a job close to Rick and an apartment. That moved me one hour away from planning headquarters. And chaos.

One Saturday, Mom and Dad came up to visit so we could find my bridesmaids' dresses. After we accomplished our mission, we decided to have lunch at Big Boy's restaurant. We had a nice time sitting there, our mouths full of burger, though Mom did seem a little off. After we finished eating, she turned to Dad and said, "Could you leave us alone for a minute?" Dad obliged, leaving the table. Mom and I remained. What was going on?

"Janene," she said, a slight tremble in her voice. "I know you've been very busy. But I've been busy, too, and all this wedding planning? Though fun, it has been quite a strain. I'll be honest. I think I'm starting to lose it."

"I'm so sorry!" I said, and I was. "I didn't realize, Mom. Tell me, what can I do?"

Her eyes grew wet as she grabbed my hand and gave it a fierce squeeze. Then a tear rolled down her cheek as she said, "Dammit, I WANT THE FRUIT CUP!"

For a moment I just sat there, shocked. The fruit cup? Then I couldn't help but laugh. She couldn't help but laugh, too. It was just so funny. Mom hadn't started to lose it. She'd *lost* it. I couldn't blame her, though. She'd been working so hard with everything going on. Right then and there I decided if she wanted a fruit cup, so it would be.

When the wedding finally came and the fruit cups were served, were the bananas brown? Yep. But I didn't care. My mom was happy and that made me happy, too.

It was an awesome wedding. :)

Oh, that day. There'd been so much planning, but it did turn out to be grand -- make that a few grand. Actually, a little more. Weddings can be expensive. Just ask my father. In fact, I still remember the stack of business cards the reception hall gave to him. He passed them out at the wedding and got a few chuckles as well as some all-too-knowing nods. They said:

> *I didn't pick out the dress. I didn't pick out the flowers.*
> *I didn't pick out the ring.*
> *This reception hall? I didn't pick it out, either.*
> *I'm just paying for the whole darn thing!*

Ah, yes. He paid for it with money. Mom and I paid for it in blood, sweat, and tears. The easiest part was picking out the dress, something I hadn't expected.

We walked into the first (make that only) bridal shop and were led straight into a dressing room. The salesgirl asked what kind of dress I liked as she gave me a quick once over. Then she told us to wait a second or two while she visited the big bad bridal closet in the back.

She returned with an armload of dresses, but I'd already picked out the one I wanted. It was on the girl in the dressing room across from me. I saw her wearing it and told Mom, "That's it." When the sales girl came back, I pointed to the girl in the dress and said, "That's the one. As soon as she takes it off, bring it in here. Which she did.

When I tried it on and I swear I heard the angels sing. It wasn't that expensive, either. Thank goodness, because the alterations were. Like people say, it's all in the details. Well, the details cost an arm and an inseam.

Oh, by the way, before I move on did I mention what my sister, Heather, had on the menu when she married a few years later? You guessed it. French onion soup and I have to say, it was delicious.

## THE MOTHER LOAD

Wait! Did you see what I did back there? That French onion soup comment was a (hopefully) funny dig at my mom. Can you believe it? Even when it comes to me, moms get no respect. So why do we do it? Why do we subject ourselves to what seems to be a lifetime of misery? I'll be honest. I'd have never become a mom had I known just how difficult it would be. Thank goodness no one ever told me. Call me a masochist, but I love being a mom. It's not all sunshine and roses but there are good times. In fact, some times are downright great. It's like riding a roller coaster. The kiddie ones that putt-putt in a circle are no fun at all. Give me the twists, loops and barrel rolls. Sure there are the lows but, man, the highs!

There are so many highs.

Your child's first smile. When they run to you when they have a boo boo because Mom's kisses are magic. When the first thing they do after scoring that goal is look for your face in the crowd. Sharing their secrets and fears -- things they won't tell anyone else because no one understands quite like you. Achieving that one goal they'd worked so hard for, only to turn to you and say, "Thanks for helping, Mom. I couldn't have done it without you." (Okay, that last thing never happened to me, but it did give you a warm, fuzzy feeling, didn't it?)

Plus there is laughter. Oh, the laughter! Kids really do say the funniest things. To prove, I'm ending this chapter with jewels straight from the lips of my kids. I hope they make you smile.

**One of my kids at age THREE**, when asked the question: "What time do you eat breakfast?" The answer: "Daytime."

**One of my kids at age FOUR**, when caught with a muddy stick, smearing muddy stripes on Grandma and Grandpa's dog: "I'm painting. What a masterpiece!"

**One of my kids at age FIVE**, while at the dinner table rattling off words that begin with 'f':

"Father…frost…feather…fum…"

"Fum?" I reply. "Don't you mean 'fun'?"

"No." Lifts a thumb high in the air. "Fum!"

**One of my kids at age SIX**, when told that money doesn't buy happiness: "But money buys ice cream, and ice cream makes me happy."

**One of my kids at age SEVEN**, while handing me a stuffed teddy bear: "Here, Mom. I poured all of my love into this. Keep it so when I'm away you can still feel my love." Aw!

**One of my kids at age EIGHT**, confessing that they told someone our family secret: "What secret?" I asked. The kid's reply: "The fact that we're all crazy."

**One of my kids at age NINE**, right on their birthday: "I can't believe it. Half of my childhood is over."

**One of my kids at age (a little after) TEN**, when told he's flirting with danger. "Flirting, mom? I'm *dating* it!"

**One of my kids at age ELEVEN**, "I can read your mind, Mom. I must be psychotic!"

## ViOLeNT aCT of RaNDoMNeSS!

***You're Psychic!*** *-- May 11, 2012*
Oh my god, you're psychic! How do I know? Just look at this:

> **My Mind**

See? **You just read my mind!** The proof is RIGHT THERE.

Sorry, that was silly. I do have some real proof, though. Just open your mind and guess which photo is going to appear below. Is it...

a) a purse
b) a tree
c) a car, OR
d) a double-yolked egg I cracked open last week that looks just like a butt?

Once you think you've got the answer, continue.



Keep going...



...almost there...

Ta da! IT'S THE PURSE!

**I'm kidding.** It's the butt egg.

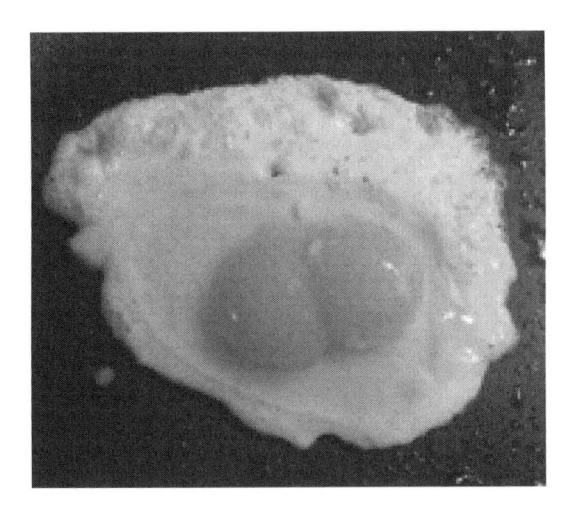

I just couldn't resist...but you knew that, didn't you? ;) I rest my case.

Psychic.

# CHAPTER 5
## There's Something Wrong with Me

I understand that I think a bit differently than most people. Case in point: yogurt. It upsets me that, even though it's supposed to be "cultured," it always spits in my face when I peel back the foil on the container.

Plus I obsess about words. Right now I'm fixated on "phlegm." I think it wins the trifecta for not only looking and sounding gross but also representing something gross, too. Plus I think about what it would be like if we took words literally. If my cat really had my tongue, I'd be upset. And what about requests? When I asked my husband what he wanted on his birthday cake he said, "Just put 'Happy Birthday, Rick.' Nothing fancy." So that's what I told the bakery to do.

He laughed, though I don't understand why. That's what he asked for, isn't it? Hmmm.

I also think about pails. I must admit I feel sorry for them. Unless you're building a sandcastle, you never ask for one. You always go for a bucket. It always rains in buckets and, if you're loaded, you've got buckets of money. When you die, you don't kick the pail. Alas, to always be considered the wimpy, effeminate cousin of the bucket. They pale in comparison.

I also wonder who came up with the idea of fork-splitting English muffins. The whole concept seems unusual to me. Also, the concept of forking a muffin sounds more than a little dirty to me.

But now that we're far enough into this book, I feel it's time to do more than just expose my quirks. I think you're ready to learn a little more about my unseemly side. All this wisdom I've been spouting should be taken with a grain of salt. Why? Because I'm a fraud. The whole wonderful mother, friend and conscientious citizen thing? Smoke and mirrors, baby.

In fact, when you get right down to it, I've been a liar, a cheater and a thief. That's right, all three. Unfortunately, I've never been good at any of them, as proven by the stories below. But why tell you when I can show you. Let's jump into the details of my criminal past. Just promise not to judge. I've learned from my mistakes and, though I doubt it, you might just learn something, too.

### NO NERVES OF STEAL

We'll start with my role as a thief. I started young -- the tender age of six. The scene of the crime was a garage sale. I'll be honest (ha!) the details are a little fuzzy. I don't remember the exact location. All I remember was strolling along the sidewalk with nary a care on my mind and School House Rock's "Conjunction Junction" on my lips. I passed a long, cement driveway with a gentle slope upward. At the top? The aforementioned garage sale. It was a bustle of activity. No one was paying any attention to the little girl sixty feet away on the sidewalk. So when a tiny rubber ball with a sticker that said "5 cents" on it rolled down to her, no one glanced.

That little girl was me. I picked up the rubber ball and gave it a bounce on the ground. So satisfying. I *needed* that ball. I just *had* to have it. Unfortunately, I had no money.

Five cents…why five cents? It was such a pittance, yet so much for a rubber ball. WAY too much, in fact. How dare they charge that kind of money! They should be punished for their greed!

I jammed the ball in the front pocket of my Tough Skins, then hustled home. It was mine -- all mine! But the exhilaration soon faded. I had sullied my soul for a stupid piece of nothing.

Was this the type of person I was -- who I wanted to be? Stealing was wrong. In one fast, bold move I'd become a felon. A lawbreaker. A thief.

And it killed me. A tortured soul was I. I'd never broken the law before. I was better than that. I had to make things right. I went back to the garage sale.

And it was over. What could I do? I decided to throw the ball up the driveway. The ball sputtered near the door to the garage then rolled back down toward me. Curses. I threw it again. It returned. Again. This went on for a good long while. I don't know what tired first, my arm or my patience, but I was done. I couldn't throw it anymore. The thought of just leaving it in the grass where it would have stayed never dawned on me. Like I said, I'm a dork.

What happened next? Just as I moved to set the ball down at the bottom of the driveway, I heard a woman call out, "Sweetie? Was that you throwing something at my garage?" I froze --not for long though, just enough to see a bewildered woman hanging out of the house's front door. Then I ran -- *fast* -- fueled with the desperate hope that she couldn't pick me out of a line up. As silly as the situation was, I never stole again. I had learned my lesson.

But when it came to cheating, that was another issue entirely.

## HOLDING MYSELF ACCOUNTABLE

I did it just once, a fact that some people find hard to believe. The truth is cheating felt so foreign to me. I never understood why people did it. That whole bit about 'if you cheat, you're only cheating yourself'? I believed it. It served me well, too. I studied hard and learned a lot. When there's a trivia contest, people want me on their team. Woo hoo! However, when I took Accounting II in college I absolutely hit the wall. There were so many formulas -- ones I knew I'd never use -- and I was fried when finals finally rolled around.

So I did it. I cheated. In the lightest of pencil, I wrote a formula I'd had trouble remembering onto my calculator. I know. It doesn't sound like much, but it was a lot to me. I'd gone through fourteen years of schooling without one act of academic trickery. It was a source of pride. Now that pride was gone. Like a small chip in a beautiful vase, I no longer felt perfect. I felt awfully scared, too.

During the test, a guy five rows up from me was caught cheating. Holy guacamole!

So here's the point in the story where I should add some sort of thought-provoking line meant to sway kids from cheating. Problem is, I don't know what to say. Some people cheat and some don't. All I know is it didn't work for me. Cheating made me feel like a person I didn't want to be. Plus it almost gave me a heart attack. Sure the guilt was self-inflicted, but there's one person in the world I hate to disappoint more than anyone: myself.

Which leads me to My Big Fat Lie. (Does the capitalization make it look sinister?) I felt like such a winner after that whole debacle. Truth be told, it wasn't huge. No one was harmed by my words, unless you want to count my ego. In fact, like with most cases of lying, when I first told it I thought it wasn't a big deal at all. Unfortunately, that assumption ended up being wrong. Totally wrong.

### LIAR, LIAR, PANTYHOSE ON FIRE

Let me take you back to the summer of 1989, the year I graduated college. I had graduated from one of the best business programs in the country -- with honors, no less. I also had no job, in part because I hadn't really looked for a job during my senior year. Mistake. I should have studied a little less and pounded the pavement more. What's worse, I could have stayed another year in school and gotten a master's degree. But I didn't. I couldn't wait to take the business world by storm!

It was more like a sprinkle.

Anyway, right after college I moved back in with my folks. While looking for a job, I worked as a temp. For five months, I took the Metra train to downtown Chicago to play secretary. It was a bit embarrassing. By that time, I had expected to do great things. So when a cute guy sat next to me on the bus to my office, I lied.

Side note (a.k.a. my excuse): I was engaged to my husband, Rick, at the time. I didn't need complications. I thought the guy on the bus was just hitting on me. More importantly, I didn't think I'd see him again.

So this guy sits next to me and asks me what I do. I tell him I'm a graduate student. I'm just working as a temp until the school year starts again. No biggie. He bought it without a problem.

Much to my ~~regret~~ surprise, I saw him often on the bus. Many times we sat together. It wasn't anything major, just two people enjoying each other's chit chat. Turns out, he wasn't some letch who wanted a piece of me. Then the feces hit the fan. It happened one day in late September. He scrunched his eyebrows and cocked his head.

"Hey, shouldn't you be back in school by now?"

Boy, did my cheeks turn red. I couldn't keep up the charade. That's when I told him the real story. (Cue the violins...)

I told him how I had graduated in May and was currently living with my parents. I'd been working as a temp as I tried to get my life in order. I poured my heart out to him, explaining how I'd lied because I was embarrassed about my situation. The whole bit about being a graduate student? How I wish that had been true. I had made a mistake. I should have stayed in school. He listened without saying a word.

After I finished telling him my tale of woe, he just sat back and stared at me for a while. I was so nervous. What would he say? Would he forgive me? Tell me it was okay? How he understood?

He finally spoke. "You know, if you had told me the truth from the beginning I wouldn't have thought you were a loser. But you didn't and now that I know you lied, I do. A total loser."

What can I say? My life ain't all comedy, folks. I felt the lowest of low.

So there you have it -- my criminal past as a liar, cheater, and a thief. I sucked at all three. Even if I had been a pro at any of them, I couldn't have continued. The feelings were just too heavy.

Except lying. If you've been following me for a while, you'll know my saying I only lied once isn't true. Once again, I see the irony of that statement, but I'm going to let it slide. Even in this book, remember how I lied to my ex-boyfriend about meeting the guy I was going to marry? Though it wasn't a lie, I didn't know that at the time so, to me, I had told an untruth.

Most people tell little white lies now and again. I am no exception. There are some people, though, that take lying to a whole new level. Enter the Botox mom.

**BABY'S GOT BOTOX**
Back in 2011 there was this crazy pageant mom who gave Botox treatments to her eight year-old daughter. Well, if you watched the news you know the story didn't end there. A few days after the story broke, Child Protective Services removed the daughter from the

woman's custody until further investigation. The mom panicked, explaining the story was all a hoax she had fabricated to make some money. She said the reporter who originally wrote the story was in on it, too. The reporter called the mom a liar, saying she believed it to be true -- she even saw the woman give her daughter the Botox injections!

Who's telling the truth? We may never know but we do know *somebody* lied. So why do people do it? In the case above it may have been for money, to get a child back, or sell some newspapers. There are many other reasons, of course. People lie to get things, like a job, or get rid of things, like a used car. They may want to make someone feel good, or make them feel bad. They might also be lazy, afraid, or want to cover their butt.

Whatever the reason, everyone has to acknowledge lying comes with risk. If you lie, you can lose respect, someone's trust, as well as a lot of sleep. You can also lose that job, get sued for that car and, under certain circumstances, there's even jail. When you go down a road of lies you never know exactly where you'll end up.

*I meant that figuratively, not literally. Sheesh!*

But enough of the lecture. You're probably wondering about moms. Do they ever lie? Well...I've got to be honest with you. If I said I never lied it would be a big fat fib. Here are some examples of my dishonesty:

**Confession #1:** The pacifier fairy did not come and take my son's last binky away. I took it out from under his pillow, tossed it into a bonfire in a fit of joy, and replaced it with a Thomas the Tank Engine story book.

*My reasoning:* Fear he would hang onto my pant leg for days, tears streaming down his face, begging for his binky back. Fairies have a strict "no take backs" rule and are conveniently unavailable during times of weakness. Strangely, kids get that, even at a very young age.

**Confession #2:** That chicken I made last night? In truth I did make it the exact same way I made it four months ago.

*My reasoning:* Frustration, exhaustion, and certainty that if my kids really -- I mean *really* -- gave it a try this time they might have liked it.

Oh, and while I'm coming clean here, the crust is not -- I repeat NOT -- the best part of the sandwich. Moms say that because not eating the crust is a waste of food. Plus the crust has eight times more pronyl-lysine (an antioxidant that raises phase 2 enzyme levels which helps prevent cancer) than the white part, and has more fiber, too. Even though it's not the best part, it's still a pretty dang good part so, come on, EAT YOUR CRUST. By the way, if you think I knew that whole antioxidant thing off the top of my head you are wise beyond your years. I am that smart. Really. ;)

I asked a huge group of kids (four) what they considered to be the biggest lie parents told them. They all agreed it was the one about kids being able to grow up to be president. What? No, "where do babies come from?" I blame the sample size. Well, anyway, as it relates to the whole president thing, all I can say is this: Many of our presidents came from humble beginnings. You really never know. Someone has to be president, right? Why *couldn't* it be one of them? Plus, there's this awesome quote, too:

> *"When you reach for the stars you might not quite get one, but you won't come up with a handful of mud, either."*
> **- Leo Burnett**

One of a mom's most important jobs is to encourage their kids, give them the confidence to pursue their dreams. It's a tough world out there, dontcha know. Having someone in your corner makes a difference.

So, yes, sometimes moms might lie but they do it with the best of intentions.

Honest.

### Madre Herald

**Boy makes face, stays that way**

Mom says, 'told him so'

Swearing linked to cancer

A little while ago, I had to dole out a punishment to one of my kids for a particularly grievous crime. When they whined, wondering why the punishment was so stiff, I told them the truth: I was on a sugar rush from too many Twinkies, thus impairing my decision-making skills.

Okay, so that wasn't really the truth. My kid knew it, too. But it killed me that they were more upset about their punishment than atoning for their sins. It's important for kids to take responsibility for their actions, be they good or bad. As for me spouting off about my Twinkie problem, that's totally my father's fault.

You see, not *all* parents lie with a good purpose in mind. Some do it just to mess with you. Take my dad. He's a jokester who enjoys telling tall tales. One time it bit him in the butt. To illustrate, allow me to present a tale called *Dad and Ronald Reagan*. It's my family's *Peter and the Wolf*.

### PBJ AND RONALD REAGAN

One Saturday when I was six or so, my dad made me a peanut butter and jelly sandwich. I told him I was tired of PBJ. Mom had made them for lunch all week. He responded, "Mine are better. In fact, they're the best in the world. I'm the PBJ making champion. I won a medal and everything."

And I believed him.

Now you might say that little anecdote says more about me than about him. I was a gullible kid. I was also six and never thought my dad would lie to me. Still, when I announced at the school lunch table that my dad was a champion PBJ maker, all the kids started laughing at me. I put two and two together.

As I grew older, I got even wiser. My fellow siblings did, too. When Dad told us we'd eaten monkey meat after leaving a Chinese restaurant, we just rolled our eyes. When he said he'd seen Sasquatch during our trip to Colorado, we didn't believe him then, either.

We got used to his antics, often enjoying his attempts to pull one over on us. Then something happened that changed his ways. **He told the best tall tale EVER.**

It was 1980, the year Ronald Reagan ran against Jimmy Carter for the U.S. presidency. We were sitting around the dinner table talking about the election when Dad announced, "I sat in Ronald Reagan's lap." All of us looked at Dad and laughed. How did he come up with this stuff? Unabashed, he continued with his story. We humored him and listened.

Back in 1950, when he lived in Chicago, his family won a contest claiming them "The Typical American Family." One of the prizes was a loving cup, long since broken and thrown away. Another was a home visit from the cast of *Louisa*, a movie in which Ronald Reagan starred. Dad was seven at the time, and as cute as can be. Ronald Reagan strolled through their apartment's front door. "He plunked down in your grandpa's chair, sat me on his knee, and told me stories. It was cool."

*Yeah*, we thought, *too cool to be true*. Dad swore to us he wasn't lying but he'd told so many stories over the years. How could we believe him? For months he held firmly to his version of events. For months we just shook our heads. Then one day my father had had enough. I still remember that day.

I don't know how he got them. They must have been buried in one of Grandma's drawers -- pictures, plus a newspaper article, too. He slapped them on the kitchen counter. Whoa. We stood there, completely amazed. Dad had been telling the truth.

*There he is! My dad sitting on Reagan's lap!*

I can't say Dad's stories ended after that. He still loved to pull our legs. In fact, he still does -- to his grandkids, too -- and, you know, I love him for it. He doesn't string us along like he used to do, though. He says he's kidding right away. And when we ask for the truth, he always tells it...at least I think he does.

Still, I have to say his love for pulling our legs did make my years growing up a bit of a challenge. I still remember when I got my first two-wheeler on my fourth (or fifth?) birthday. How I loved it so. It was purple, with pink and white streamers bursting from the handle bars. Yep, I was stylin' on the sidewalk. That is, I *would* be stylin'. First, I had to learn how to ride it.

### A HEFTY PRICE TO PAY

Alas, my dad teaching me how to ride a bike. That's an interesting tale. We started off in cute movie montage style -- me, pedaling furiously, while he ran alongside me shouting words of encouragement. I still remember the scary thrill when he'd give me that last push before he let go. It took many tries before it finally happened -- I totally wiped out.

After the moment of initial shock wore off, I looked down at my legs. One of them had a huge, bloody scrape. A tear trickled down my cheek.

Who am I kidding? I bawled with big boo-hoo tears and a howl that could be heard throughout the land. Running over, Dad scooped me up and brought me back over to the house. Placing me on the hood of his car, he frowned as he assessed the situation.

"Hmmm..." he said. "It looks bad. Really bad."

What? That didn't help at all!

I cried louder. I was dying, I tell you -- a fact my dad practically confirmed! Then my dad went into the garage and came out with two things: a Hefty bag and an axe.

"I'm afraid the leg has to come off," he said.

My tears immediately dried up. "No, no, no," I said. "It's not that bad. Honest!"

"Can you walk on it?"

"I know I can! Just give me a chance!"

He shook his head. "Well, okay. Let's see."

Channeling my best Meryl Streep, I hopped off the hood and walked straight into the house. Then I ran under my bed and hid for five hours so my dad couldn't find me -- or did we go out for ice cream? I have to admit, some facts are easier to remember than others.

Now that I'm done throwing my dad under the bus, I think it's only fair that I do the same for me. Although, we already know I'm not that great at lying, cheating, or thievery, there is something that I'm good at. I'm vain.

## PICTURE PERFECT

Until I had kids, I refused to go anywhere without make up. During college, I would actually put on my mascara while in bed. Three coats. (I have thin lashes.)

Like I mentioned before, I'm like a lot of females -- always worried about my looks. It's sad, really, though I didn't realize how sad until a little while ago. It started when one of my friends changed her Facebook profile pic to a cute photo of her family. I wrote on her wall, "I love your profile pic. Everyone looks so good!" She replied, "Well you never pick a bad one, do you???"

Hmm. Excellent point.

Then another one of my friends chimed in saying she was tempted to change her profile pic to something hideous. Of course, knowing how crazy and fun she was, I wasn't surprised when she ended up doing just that. Minutes later, a goofy photo of her appeared.

I laughed. "Game on," I posted on her wall. I dug into our computer archives. An awful photo of me had to be somewhere in there. Well, guess what? I couldn't find one.

That's right. After scrolling through thousands of photos, I couldn't find even one where I looked bad. Sound conceited? I wasn't. The truth was much sadder. I was way too vain.

Over the years, I'd hide from being in pictures by always being the one who took them. Whenever I *was* in a picture and I thought I looked bad, I'd delete it, no questions asked. I'd think, "No big deal. A lot of people do it." And that's true, but here's the thing with me: in the 3000+ photos we had on our family computer, I was only in 60.

Yep. I was in less than 2% of our photos. What a legacy.

Granted, I've always been the cameraman. During trips and family gatherings it's usually me taking the photos. Still, that 2% statistic really stunk and it was because I had to look perfect all the time. In my quest to look flawless for future generations, I quite literally cut myself out of the picture.

It made me wonder what had spurred me to delete so many photos of myself. Could I have had that many bad hair days? Does my smile keep looking crooked or my eyes keep drooping or did the photos just look like the real me instead of the idealized one I had in my head?

Well, from that moment on, I stopped discarding every bad photo of myself. Life isn't perfect and neither was I. My friends and family loved me the way I am. Why couldn't I love myself?

Years from now, when I have a grandchild in my lap and we're looking at old family photos, I may not look great but at least I'll be there. Present.

In the picture.

*photo number 61*

So obviously, I am not perfect though, somehow I get the feeling you already knew that.

Regardless, I felt the need to announce this very fact. I gave a full confession after I'd neglected to post on my blog for a couple of weeks. Shame on me. I felt such pressure to write something. I was letting tens of readers down! In truth, they probably didn't care. The person I felt I'd really let down was myself. Still I had nothing in my head to write. Sure, a few seeds had been planted. They just wouldn't germinate. Like the road sign I had come across a few weeks prior. I should have been able to make a joke about that.

*Seriously?*

But I couldn't. My mind had been cluttered. There'd been so much going on at the time. And as much as I wanted people to believe I had it all together, I just didn't.

That made me think of Sturgis, the yearly motorcycle festival in South Dakota. Years back when my family was on the road during vacation we saw a man on a motorcycle. He was huge, with tattooed arms, a shaved head and a scraggly beard. Simply put, he looked scary. That is, until we saw the back of his motorcycle. Then we had to giggle. There, attached with duct tape, was a cardboard sign that said, "Stoogis or bust."

Yep. You read that right. *Stoogis*. It's hard to look like a badass when you make a mistake like that.

I have to admit, when I see people goof up like that, I feel better about myself. Not in an "I'm better than you" kind of way, but more of a "looks like I'm not the only one who doesn't have life all figured out."

We all have struggles, things we don't want others to know lest they judge us as less than absolutely perfect. In our society it's so important that people see us as having our lives under total control. I feel such pressure to be the perfect mom, perfect friend, perfect writer, perfect wife. And I'm not. Not even close. I don't have all the answers. Heck, I don't even know all of the questions.

So if you ever feel like you don't measure up, don't worry. You're in good company. It's rare to find someone who thinks they've got life all figured out, and those people are usually jerks.

Just keep on plugging and do the best that you can. That's all anyone can ask. If you make a mistake, I might giggle, but I'll also forgive you. Promise me you'll do the same.

## ViOLeNT aCT of RaNDoMNeSS!
### CALAMITY LANE

It's amazing how what you grow up with seems so normal, even when it's crazy. Take commuting to my job. When I lived in the suburbs of Chicago but worked in the city, it took me an hour and a half to get to work. I drove ten minutes to the train station, spent ten minutes waiting at the train station, forty-five minutes sitting on the train, five minutes walking to my bus once I got off the train, five minutes waiting for the bus, ten minutes on the bus, then an additional ten walking the rest of the way, riding the elevator, etc. until I finally got to my desk. And this was normal. A lot of people, like me, did it every day.

Even when I stopped working in the city, I had crazy commutes. Illinois I-294 tollway? I know it very well. My car put on a lot of miles and I logged a lot of hours -- especially when there'd been an accident. Traffic jams were the worst.

Usually, when there'd been an accident up ahead, by the time my car finally reached the scene most of the damage had been cleaned up. Except one time. I'll never forget it. It really made my hair stand on end.

I can't remember the date. I can't even remember the road. I just remember what I saw. Like most accidents, traffic was backed up a bit from the accident scene. All I could do was creep along and look for signs of what had happened.

It started with a long red, splatter in the middle of the road. My stomach lurched. Then I saw another one about fifty yards up. What had happened here? Beginning to shake, I looked ahead. All I saw were flashing lights from three police cars parked behind a white semi truck -- one of the truck's door hung there, ajar. Oh, man, an accident involving a semi. Not a good sign.

Traffic continued to inch forward. As I got closer to the scene, more and more splatters and streaks of red appeared on the pavement. I made a promise to myself. When I came up onto the scene, I wouldn't look. I didn't want to know.

But I did look. I don't know what it is about the human condition. We're just so curious. I couldn't help but watch intently as a policeman directed cars -- including mine -- to the outside lane. Other people -- some policemen, others not -- donned gloves as they scurried to clean up the scene. What exactly were they picking up off the road? I hoped to God it wasn't body parts. Then I looked inside the truck and noticed what lay within: huge palette of cans -- cans filled with Heinz tomato paste. One of the palettes had burst through the door and fallen off the truck.

The red splatters I had seen? Tomato paste. When the cans hit the pavement they had exploded on impact. Whew! I sat back in my seat and chuckled. Then I cursed.

Man, I hated traffic jams.

# CHAPTER 6
# Lost in Translation

The places I've seen! The things I have done!

That's right, I've traveled a bit. My tales of woe and stupidity don't all stem from the U.S.A. I've played the fool everywhere. And how did I come to travel so much? Simple: The U.S. Army.

Shortly after Rick finished school, we decided to take the plunge. We were living in Milwaukee, Wisconsin at the time and couldn't wait to see where the Army would take us. Italy? Japan? It ended up being even better. It was Fort Sheridan, Illinois! A cute little post north of Chicago, it lay right on Lake Michigan's shoreline. It was also fifteen minutes from my hometown. From Rick's hometown, a whopping thirty.

Which was fine. Honestly. Not only could I keep my high-stress, low-paying job but revel in the fact that my commute to that job tripled. Plus we got to go to every family get-together. Every. Single. One.

Okay, I've got to call BS on myself. I loved being around my family. I loved my job, too. Kind of. Sort of. In the beginning. It blew large, stinking chunks near the end. But I got another job and, lo and behold, once I did they closed Fort Sheridan six months later. You see, the Army has a rule: once you're settled in, it's time to move on. Before we knew it, we were off to Germany!

Now before I tell you my travelling tales, you must know that when I said I'd played a fool everywhere I was joking. In fact, I know what you've been thinking as you've been reading this book: "How did this woman get so wise?" Well, I could tell you that with age comes wisdom and, after many years of parenting, I've learned a thing or two. But the truth of the matter is I've been wise all my life. I came out of the womb filled with shrewd sensibilities.

Also important to note before I tell this first tale is the fact that I studied Spanish in school. To my delight I became quite fluent, allowing me to travel to Mexico several times without fear of accidentally ordering flaming donkey hooves with my chicken enchiladas. As for traveling during our three year-stint in Germany, it didn't scare me one bit. Here's the story:

### VISITING THE WALL -- WHAT A BLAST!

We moved there during the summer of 1993, not long after The Wall came down. If you don't know about The Wall, read the gratuitously educational section shown below. If you do know, just hop over it.

*When World War II ended in 1945, Europe was divided into two separate groups: the NATO countries and the Warsaw Pact countries. Germany was the only country split in two, turning it into East Germany and West Germany. I know that was mean, but for some strange reason everyone was pretty mad at the Germans and didn't care.*

*Anyway, the NATO countries all had democratic governments, whereas the Warsaw Pact countries were tied to the Soviet Union, which was run by communists. Dirty, filthy communists! World War II had just ended, and already the Cold War had begun. Sigh.*

*What was the Cold War? Well, it wasn't really a war, just a lot of tension, worry, and name-calling between the two sets of countries. This not only produced some totally awesome thriller spy movies, but the Berlin Wall -- a tall, cement wall that separated East Berlin from West Berlin -- and the "Iron Curtain" -- a long, heavily guarded steel (not iron!) fence that separated the Eastern/Warsaw Pact countries from the Western/NATO ones. If the countries couldn't play nice, they wouldn't play at all! Built by the Soviets, its main purpose was to keep Easterners in and Westerners out.*

*Now I won't get into all of the politics, but I will tell you that people COULD NOT CROSS THAT FENCE. Military, diplomats, tourists from afar? Only through special checkpoints and if they had the right paperwork. Everyday citizens? No way. If they tried -- and some from the oppressive East side did – the Soviet guards were under orders to shoot them on sight. That's the way things remained until 1989 when Soviet leadership crumbled and both the Wall and Iron Curtain were torn down.*

Okay, history lesson over. It's time to get back to my tale of infinite wisdom...

We were stationed about twenty miles from the old East German/West German border in a town called Schweinfurt.

(Translation: Pig Crossing. No joke.) We decided it'd be cool to drive up to the old border patrol checkpoints and see what was left. The short answer: not much. Aside from an old tank trail and some heavy metal fencing, little of the area remained. Here's a photo (and yes, that's my husband looking all serious):

Even though there wasn't much to see, it was cool traipsing through the grass field, imagining what life was like just a few short years ago.

Oh! I forgot to mention something else we saw. Posted sporadically in the field were small white signs in German. What did they say? Don't ask me. Like I said, I knew Spanish, not German. So we did what most Americans do in a foreign country. We ignored them.

Flash forward three years. Our tour in Germany was wrapping up. We decided to go back to the border and see how much it had changed. The short answer: again, not much. But *I* had changed. I was not only pregnant, but fairly fluent in German. Hey, what do you know! I could read the signs!

Now my German is not what it used to be, so I'll have to paraphrase, but they said a little something like this:

*Attention*
*Danger!*
*Entering and walking the field is forbidden!*

Then they went on to inform us there were yet to be diffused landmines buried throughout the area.

*LANDMINES?*

It took us half an hour to walk the forty foot stretch back to our car.

Anyway, like I said, I've been wise all my life. Any other questions? If not, I've got another mildly entertaining tale about The Wall for you to read.

### DOWN IN THE DUMPSTER

Rick and I took a trip to Berlin. It was 1994, five years after the Berlin Wall came down -- well, *started* to come down. You've got to remember, the thing measured 103 miles long and twelve feet wide. That's a lot of concrete, and all along the former border were dumpsters filled with it.

That was even the case when we visited Checkpoint Charlie, the former crossing point between East and West Berlin. It looked nothing like a tourist attraction. In fact, little had changed from the days of Soviet occupation. Stranger yet, we were the only ones there. Okay, that's not quite true. There was someone else.

I'll just call him an opportunist from the East. He stood behind a folding table. After we looked around, we went up to his table -- an old metal one with rickety legs. Colorful pieces of concrete sat on top, all of them stamped "Official Berlin Wall" and marked for sale. Well, Rick and I aren't stupid. Well, maybe we are but that's beside the point. Both of us immediately suspected that this guy might not be above board. For all we knew, the chunks on the table were not from the wall. They could have come be from anywhere. Then we looked at the edge of the parking lot and saw three dumpsters brimming with Wall.

Sure, we could have just grabbed an eighty pound hunk from a dumpster and be done with it. But it would have looked awfully silly on our fireplace mantle, plus I'm a klutz. It would have landed on my foot. So, instead, we purchased a much smaller piece from our fortune-seeking friend. Was it fake? We didn't know, but any guy who felt the need to haul counterfeit concrete into a demolition zone probably needed a buck or two.

### A HAIR RAZING EXPERIENCE

Now for some idiocy. Let me set the scene: June, 1993. We had only been living in Germany one month and I knew desperately little about the country. Rick's parents had come to visit. We decided to travel to the Black Forest, which wasn't really black but a deep dark green. And kind of touristy.

Our hotel was cute and very German. Only one person, a cook, knew any English. When we arrived I was starving. Still, beauty came first. As soon as I walked into our room I plugged in my curling iron. There's nothing like freshly curled bangs when you're about to go down on a Jaeger schnitzel.

Like I said, we were new to German living and I'd yet to learn the ins and outs of their electric power. I did know it was different. Instead of 110 volts, they use 220. In simple terms, their power runs twice as hot. Also -- and this point is important -- their plugs are two round metal prongs instead of rectangles. Fortunately, I had a thingy that allowed you to plug an American appliance into a German outlet. Only it didn't convert the power. So when I inserted my

American plug into a German socket, I'd created a weapon. Maybe it wasn't enough to blow up a bunker, but it sure could sizzle my bangs.

Which it did. Thinking nothing of the hotter than usual instrument of beauty I held in my hands, I wrapped my hair around the barrel and heard a sizzle. Then my bangs were gone. Okay, they weren't gone. They were still there, only they weren't attached to my head. Instead, they were attached -- nay, they were *glued* -- to my poor little curling iron.

When I pulled the barrel (and my bangs) from my forehead, I couldn't help but laugh at myself. It wasn't the first time I'd done something stupid. I had another story to tell. Was I embarrassed? Absolutely, but I took comfort in the fact that only a few people would know what I'd done.

And I was wrong. My first clue was when I heard a commotion in the hallway a few minutes later. Another minute later I heard the word "feuer!" Oh my God. Wasn't that German for "fire?" I yelled to Rick, then opened the door. Outside there were frantic people in the hallway, their noses in the air. I asked what was going on. One of them said something like, "It smells like fire!"

They had smelled my hair.

Yep, the lovely scent of scorched hair had not only filled my room, but the entire hallway. It took me a second to realize what had happened, then I ran back into my room. Grabbing my curling iron, now adorned with congealed bangs, I ran out into the hall. Then I showed them -- not one or two, but ten people -- the error of my ways.

If people say Germans never laugh, they're wrong. I heard hoots like I'd never heard before. I was no longer the only one with a tale to tell. They had a "stupid American" story, starring me.

Now on to Italy -- magnificent Italy! -- with its dangerously delectable food and even more dangerous men. At least, that's how I see it. When it comes to this next tale, the fault falls squarely on the waiter. I'm innocent!

### OUT OF ORDER

I've got to say, the history, the architecture, THE FOOD! The *Eat, Pray, Love* chick got it right. If you want to eat until your belly button pops out, Italy is the place to go. Not only does it have the best cuisine but it has the best waiters, too. In Italy, being a waiter is a vocation, not a way to help pay for college or pay the bills until some Hollywood producer discovers you. Food is an art. The chef? An artist. The server? Dang, I don't know where I'm going with this. Just trust me, Italian waiters are awesome. They strive to make your meal pleasurable, memorable.

During one of our trips to Venice, my husband and I discovered a wonderful little restaurant near Basilica di San Marco -- which sounds way cooler than St. Mark's Basilica. The atmosphere was beautiful, the menu scrumptious, the waiter? Ohhhhhh, man. Tall, dark and handsome never looked so good.

As soon as we were seated, he started rolling out the charm. That smile, that accent -- I don't care what people say, Italian is the most romantic language in the world. Though I had no idea what he was saying to me, in my heart I knew it was something like this:

> *Señorina, are you enjoying your stay in Venice? (I nod.)*
> *Never have I waited on someone so lovely. I hope you find my city lovely, too? (I nod again.)*
> *And the shopping. Please say your husband has indulged you with a trinket or two. Maybe some jewelry? A Gucci handbag? (Another nod.)*
> *Etc., etc., etc.*

And so it continued for a minute or two -- he with the questions and me nodding like a bobble-head. My husband just looked on and smiled. "Looks like I need to learn Italian," he chuckled. Well, as it turned out, *I* was the one who needed to learn it because five minutes later the waiter came out with a serving tray the circumference of the moon. I swear I saw his knees buckle right before he set it down. That's when I realized our earlier conversation had sounded more like this:

> *Señorina, would you like to start with a glass of our special house wine? (I nod.)*
> *I'm sure you would like an appetizer, as well. Can I bring you some cheese and bread to start? (I nod again.)*
> *Our salads here are also amazing. Can I interest you in our caprese salad? One for your husband, too? (Another nod)*
> *Etc., etc., etc.*

Now I can't say it was the only time I was suckered into buying something due to a language barrier, but I can say that it was the most enjoyable one. Like I said, in Italy the waiter's job is to make your dining experience memorable. He didn't fail at his task. Some of the other men I met in Italy, though, weren't quite as charming as that waiter. Take this one border guard I met on my way back to Germany. He was a stinker.

### BORDERLINE BEHAVIOR

Before I get into this next silly tale, you need to understand something about Western European borders at that time. Many were loosening. Guards no longer stopped your car, asked a zillion questions, stamped your passport then let you leave. And that sucked. I wanted my passport filled with stamps so I could brag! To do that I needed some sort of visual aid to wave in front of my less worldly friends. Luckily for me, border patrol stations stayed open. To get your passport stamped, you just had to go inside. Which I did, many times and without much ado, until I hit Italy.

Please note that after the borders relaxed, the German term for a passport stamp had changed from "stempel" ("stamp") to "souvenir." That's important to this story, plus it might help you win Double Jeopardy someday. Also note, at that time, I was wearing an off-brand polo shirt, Bermuda shorts, white bobby socks and gym shoes. Yep. I looked pretty sexy. Backward folk might even say I was asking for it.

Anyway, before Rick and I drove back into Germany, we pulled over to the border patrol station. I left Rick in the car. He already had plenty of passport stamps. (Yes, I was jealous.) Walking up to the building, I chanced upon three young male guards standing outside the door. I asked if any of them spoke English or German. "Ja," they all said. Lifting up my passport, I asked in not-so-perfect German if I could get a "souvenir." One of the guards replied, "Sorry. The station is closed for the night."

I might have pouted a little. Okay, maybe a lot. Another guard stepped forward. He looked sweet, sympathetic. "I'm so sorry, senorina. No matter. I can help you."

"You can?" I said, ignoring the devious twinkle in his eye.

"Follow me behind the building. There I'll give you a *real* souvenir of Italy."

What the…huh? Did I hear that right? He was joking, of course. The entire group broke out in laughter. I did, too, though my cheeks were awful red. So much for my "souvenir." At least I got a goofy story out of it.

But back to the Italian waiter. How I enjoyed his ~~gorgeousness~~ sweet demeanor. I must say, when it came to our experience with servers that wasn't always the case. But before I tell you *that* story, I'm going to tell you *this*. It involves our first visit to Prague. Spoiler alert: It doesn't start out so great.

## SKANKS FOR THE MEMORIES

Our first trip to Prague was in 1993, only four years after the Velvet Revolution. (If you want a history lesson on that go to Wikipedia. I'm still tuckered out from writing about The Wall and I am DONE.) To say the Czech Republic was still bouncing back after years of communism would be a big understatement. But I didn't care. My husband and I had just been stationed in Germany and I was (still am) part Bohemian -- and by Bohemian I don't mean artsy chic. I mean from Bohemia, part of the republic.

I couldn't wait to check out the motherland. We went right away. Well, you know that bit about making a good first impression? The Czech Republic failed miserably.

As soon as we drove past the border we saw dozens of (ahem) ladies of opportunity lined up along highway. And these ladies looked HARD. They were working for food, not a cute pair of Jimmy Choos. The country was in transition, all right. We feared we had arrived too early.

Many miles later, we made it to the outskirts of Prague. In order to get lodgings in the city we had to visit a shack right off the highway exit --and I do mean a shack. About ten feet square, it had clapboard walls and a concrete floor. Inside was an attendant with a bunch of binders filled with pages of make-shift hotels. There were also private residences available for rent while the tenants were away. We chose a residence -- a one-bedroom apartment for only $30 per night.

After we paid our fees and got the keys, we headed into the city. After a long search down many a broken down street, we finally found our apartment. Every building on the street was old and covered with the blackest of soot. Inside the apartment, though, we were lucky. The gentleman who resided there left us plenty of entertainment. Right next to the 13" television was a stack of pornographic magazines.

No matter. We weren't there to stay indoors, plus by then we were starving. We needed dinner. Minutes later, we put foot to pavement in search of a decent meal.

We didn't find one. When we arrived at the restaurant we had wanted to go to, it was all boarded up. It looked abandoned. (We found out later it was in the middle of being renovated. Bad timing on our part.) We searched on but all we found were more blackened buildings, torn up sidewalks and burned out streetlamps. Not ideal. In fact, it was so bad when we got back to the apartment, I considered asking Rick if he wanted to leave the next day. Little did I know, Rick was thinking the same thing. Thank goodness we didn't say anything to each other. **Because the very next day Prague became my absolute favorite city in all of Europe.**

It started the next day when our trolley -- a decrepit old thing with sparks flying everywhere -- dumped us off near the Castle District. Again, soot everywhere. I'm not exaggerating when I say the buildings were quite literally black. However, a few blocks into our walk we saw a city worker sandblasting one of them. What he uncovered amazed us. Underneath all that gunk was masterfully carved stonework -- beautiful! As we continued on our way, we saw more sand-blasted buildings, all of them absolutely gorgeous. We were inspired. Was there more to see in this town?

Abso-frickin'-lutely.

We walked down the Golden Lane at Prague Castle and explored the beautiful cathedral. We watched the Castle District light up at twilight. We found a bakery off Old Town Square that sold chocolate éclairs for just five cents a piece. FIVE CENTS! The food was crazy cheap everywhere. It was tasty, too.

The more we explored Prague, the more we loved it. We vowed to come back again and we did. In fact, we went often and each time we did, Prague got more and more beautiful. That wasn't all, though. Even the grocery store shelves which, in the beginning, were only 10% full, slowly grew increasingly stocked. It was wonderful watching the city bounce back from communist rule and return to its former glory. Each time we visited, we got bolder, going further into the country and discovering cool, new places.

I often think about what would have happened if we'd turned around and headed home that first night. I'm so glad we didn't. The Czech Republic holds such a dear place in my heart. We went back several times while living in Germany -- even one time with my parents. One day I hope to go back.

*Rick and my parents eating at famed restaurant U Fleku.*

## A BRIDGE TO ENLIGHTENMENT

Prague. Such a beautiful city. I could sit at an outdoor café for hours and just soak in the scenery. In fact, a few times I did. My favorite place to go? A cute little café right off the Charles Bridge. On the other side of the bridge stood the castle district. It was beautiful in its own right. At dusk, though, it was spectacular as they slowly illuminated sections of the district until the entire area was awash in a rainbow of colored lights.

The time when my parents came with us to Prague, we made sure they'd get a chance to view the spectacle, too. Taking no chances, we arrived at the café about an hour before the show started. The waitress greeted us kindly. She spoke no English, of course. No worries. We pointed to the menu, each of us ordering coffee or tea. She came back with our order a few minutes later. We sat, drank, and sat some more. Milking a cup of tea for so long wasn't easy, but we managed to do it. Sure, the waitress kept checking on us, but she did it sweetly, or so we all had thought. Strike that. My mom knew. She'd grown up amongst many Czech relatives. She understood the language.

So when the waitress dropped by and said something in that saccharin voice, my mom understood. And that something the waitress said near the very end wasn't as sweet as I had thought.

"Jesus Maria!" the waitress began. (Those words are kind of like Americans saying "Jesus Christ!") "So you're just going to sit there and not order anything else? Thanks for being so rude."

How did my mom respond? With a smile, of course. She pretended she hadn't understood. Why get into it with the waitress? The fact that she wanted to stay and see the show factored into it, too.

And we did see the show and it was awesome. The colored lights didn't disappoint. Plus our view was great. When we left, we made sure to leave a big tip. My mom also thanked the waitress in perfect Czech. ;)

## SLIPPERY SLOPE

Now, as much fun as we've had on the road, not all of our travels have been safe. In fact, during one trip I almost died. Luckily, I didn't. If I had, it means a ghost wrote this book, which would be creepy.

This next story took place in the loveliest of countries: Austria. It's so beautiful. Whenever I think of it, the first thing I picture is Julie Andrews twirling on top of a mountain, like she did in *The Sound of Music*. There's only one difference. Instead of singing, "The hills are alive with music," she's singing, "The hills are trying to kill you!" You'll soon learn why.

Once again, before I start you should know that I loved Swarovski crystal figurines. Every time our family goes on a trip, I get a piece to commemorate our travels. If it's a small trip, I usually get a small figurine. If it's a big trip, I get a big one. When Rick and I took a trip to Austria's Salzburg and Vienna, I bought a crystal piano to represent all the Austrian composers. Huzzah!

But back in the day, before kids, Rick and I used to travel an awful lot. If we'd purchased crystal for each trip it would have put us in the poor house. So we decided that some trips didn't warrant a crystal figurine. This was one of these trips.

Once again, it was 1993, the year we had moved to Germany. Rick was especially pumped. "We're so close to the Alps!" he would say. "I can't wait to go skiing!"

Um...yeah. Me, too? You see, I wasn't a skier. Not even a little bit. Sure, I had skied a couple of times, but both had been on small Wisconsin hills. And even then I'd sucked. We're talking black-and-blue-butt sucked. Still, Rick loved skiing. I knew I was doomed.

The first Thanksgiving we were out there, Rick made arrangements for us to go skiing with friends at Steinplatte Ski Resort in Austria. Man, was I nervous. Before we went, I told Rick I wanted lessons from a ski school instructor. Rick balked, "Lessons? You don't need no stinkin' lessons," he replied with *Blazing Saddles* flourish. Rick was an expert skier. He could easily teach me. Why throw good money away?

When we arrived at the ski lodge, I brought up the subject again. I may have even begged. "Rick, you have no idea how bad I am. I really think I need lessons."

Rick still brushed it aside. "Well, you have no idea how good a skier I am. Trust me, you'll be fine."

The next morning, after I composed my last will and testament, we suited up and hit the hills. As we rode up the chair lift, I swore the mountain grew before our eyes. It got bigger and bigger. Taller and taller. There was no way I'd make it back down. Just getting off the chair lift proved too great. As soon as I skied off the bench, I landed on my butt.

"Don't worry," Rick said with the gusto of a cheerleader trying to will their losing team to win. "Chair lifts aren't easy the first few times. You'll be fine on the hill. Just follow me."

We started going down the mountain and I did follow him for about ten seconds or so. Problem was, I didn't know how to stop or slow down. Before I knew it I was way ahead of him. And I was going fast -- too fast -- and a big turn was coming up. I screamed back to Rick, "How do I stop?" Rick bolted forward, doing his best to catch up with me. I forgot what he told me to do.

What I do remember is the mountain. You know those banked turns that keep you from skiing off a cliff? Well, this ski run didn't have one. As for those fences that catch you if you *do* run off a cliff? Nope. Didn't have those either. As I careened toward the turn I couldn't make, I realized what would happen if I didn't stop. I'd Wile E. Coyote off the cliff and then plummet to my death.

HOLY HAND GRENADES!!!!!

Rick realized it, too. "Just crash!" he yelled. Now that's something I could do well. Just shy of the cliff I tumbled backward -- a sea of arms, legs, skis and poles.

It wasn't pretty. When Rick caught up to me, a slew of creative and crude expletives burst from my mouth. He just stood there, stunned. Then he smiled at me rather sheepishly. "How would you feel about getting some lessons?"

Needless to say, I got a HUGE crystal figurine for that trip.

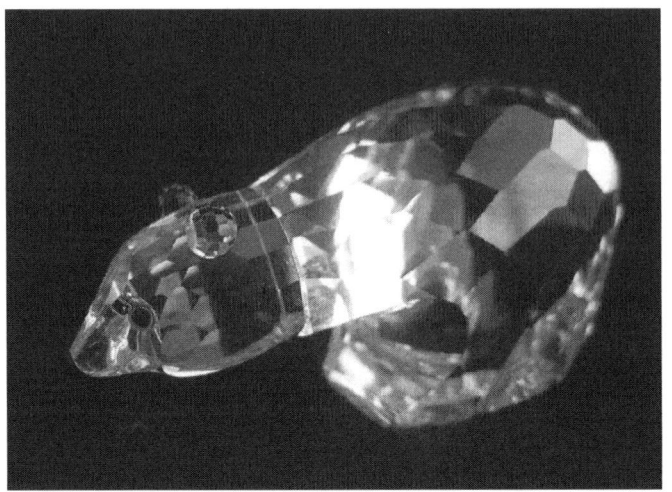

*The crystal figurine I earned for "bearing" with my husband*

## NIGHTMARE ON AMSTERDAM STREET

The only other time I felt in danger was when we visited Amsterdam. We had decided to camp. Why? I have no idea. I'd rather just blame my husband. :)

Let's begin with some travel explorations first so I can lull you into a false sense of security. We had a wonderful time in Amsterdam. It's such a gorgeous city. We cruised along the canals, saw the Anne Frank house and the coolest church hidden in an attic. Even the Red Light District was a sight to see. To put it mildly, it was (ahem) colorful. Amsterdam entranced us and kept us on our toes.

As for the camping part? It was fun. We got to meet American campers like ourselves, as well as a fun couple from New Zealand. We went to dinner together and shared our tales of European travels. Kinda cool. As for the campground, itself, it seemed safe enough. In fact, it had a seven-foot high cement wall surrounding the entire thing.

Now the question we should have asked ourselves is why the campground had that wall. If we'd spotted a hotel with a barbed wire fence surrounding it, we would have avoided the place like the plague. Well, one very early morning -- maybe 6AM or so -- I heard a commotion in our new friends' tent -- the tent that was placed no more than five feet away from ours. What was going on?

I can't remember the name of woman we befriended, so I'll just call her Gutsy. It was Gutsy's voice I heard. "Hey? What are you doing in here? Get the **** out! Then I heard shuffling...struggling. Seconds later I heard the zip of their tent flap and a person running...two people running.

Rick heard it, too. Scrambling out of our sleeping bags, we bolted from our tent. Unfortunately, or luckily, we were ten seconds too late. The only person left in Gutsy's tent was her husband, bleary-eyed and confused.

Gutsy came back a couple minutes later. She looked shaken to her core. We asked her what had happened and she told us, trembling the entire time.

Having to go to the bathroom, she had left the tent. When she came back, there was a stranger inside. It was a guy -- he'd looked totally strung out on drugs and she'd caught him going through their things. Not knowing what to do, she'd chewed him out. His eyes grew wild as he ran out of the tent. Gutsy ran after him. She was so mad and he looked so wasted, she'd wanted him captured.

But she didn't catch him, thank goodness. About one hundred feet away she saw him fall to the ground. When he did a knife popped out of his shirt. It was a big one -- one that made Freddy Krueger's finger blades look like those crappy press on nails you buy at Walgreens. That's when her bravery evaporated. Freezing, she just watched him get up, grab the knife, and jump the fence. Then she ran back to the tent.

DANG!

After she told her story, her husband went with her to report the issue to the camp office. Rick and I just stood there, stunned. That could have been us. That stranger could have entered our tent. That stranger could have used that knife. What would we have done? It didn't matter. We knew what we had to do now. Screw camping. We packed up our things.

I hope this story doesn't keep you from visiting Amsterdam in the future. It really is an awesome city. The lesson here is if you camp make sure to think twice before you do it near the drug capital of the world.

**SUIT YOURSELF**

Now not all Lost in Translation tales took place while I was overseas. Fun fact: Did you know they don't use coins on military bases in Afghanistan or Iraq? They're heavy, thus no fun to transport from the States. Military folk use laminated paper coins instead. Interesting, huh? Still, it's a fact I kind of wish I didn't know. Why? Because that means I know someone who travels to the Middle East. Shocker of shockers: it's my husband, Rick.

Not that I should worry. Rick doesn't travel there often and, when he does, he assures me he is safe. You see, Rick works for the government. When he goes there they put him behind a desk inside an office inside a metal building behind concrete blockade behind a barbed wire fence, etc. Still, I worry. Anything could happen. He could drown in a dirt storm or accidentally staple himself to death. But Rick has always done his best to assure us that he'll be okay. He'll come home safe.

Well, a while back he took that message to the extreme. He'd been tasked to Iraq for a few months. While he was gone, largely due to my insanity, I decided to host a huge family party for my son's first communion. My house was full of moms, dads, sisters, and brothers, as well as a bevy of cute nieces and nephews. They all missed Uncle Rick. My kids missed their dad. Could we Skype him? Of course! We moved my laptop to the kitchen table so all could see.

When we called, Rick was at home (a metal storage container). We laughed and joked for a little while. Then Rick said, "Hey, guys! Want to see what I look like in full battle gear?" The kids squealed, "Yes!" Rick proceeded to put on 100 pounds of gear. He looked bad ass cool. The kids oohed and ahhed, then Rick said he had to go. We ended our call and I thought that was the end of the story.

It wasn't.

What Rick hadn't told us on that sweet family day was the *reason* he'd put on all that gear. Spoiler alert: he didn't do it to impress our little crowd of pipsqueaks. Not at all.

Months later, after he was safely back at home, he told the reason he'd donned his gear. **While he'd been talking to us, the base had kind of sort of gone under attack.** "I didn't know how to explain it to the kids," he told me. "I didn't want to scare them." Or for me to freak out since he'd never mentioned attacks while he was there. When he told me that story, I wanted to hug him and throttle him at the very same time. I had to admit, it was pretty funny, given he was safely back home telling it to me in person.

But not everyone comes home. That thought is always in the back of my mind when Rick is away. Thanks goodness he's not there often, and he really is much safer than so many others over there.

The others.

There are so many people -- families, soldiers, government employees -- who have sacrificed much more than us. They are forever in my thoughts and I want them to know that.

They are my heroes.

**STARING THE OTHER WAY**

I'm sorry. I hated to end that story on a somber note, but I really wanted to include that last part. Those people really are my heroes. Still, I feel an obligation to end on a goofy note so here's what I'm going to do: I'm going to tell you one last silly snippet from my travels overseas. I'll even let you choose it. It's between:

1. The time an Irishman told me, "You can't handle the truth!"
2. The time my mother stole a train seat from a crippled lady, or
3. The time I saw French film star and airplane pisser in the aisles, Gerard Depardieu, stark naked. Maybe.

What? Seriously? You want to hear all three? I'm not sure we have the time. This is already turning into the longest chapter in the book...

Oh, all right. Let's start with the Irishman.

Rick and I were visiting the Kreutzberg Monastery. Located in Germany's Bavaria, the monks there are not known for pea plant experiments (five points to you if got that reference. If not, look up a guy named Mendel) but for brewing awesome beer. Inside the monastery was a huge, thriving bier stube full of rows and rows of wooden picnic tables. Sitting at these tables were rows and rows of happy drinkers from all over the globe. It was quite a sight to see.

One gentleman, upon hearing me speak, caught my eye and staggered over to Rick and me. Then he started talking to me in a language I couldn't decipher. What did he want with me? Raising my eyebrows, I looked at Rick and whispered, "Do you know what language that is?" Rick just laughed. "It's English with a very, very thick Irish accent. He must think you can understand him."

But I couldn't. I shrugged my shoulders while Rick intervened, good Irish-blooded man that he was. The two of them spoke for a while I just stood there, not understanding a thing. Then the guy bellowed, "You can't handle the truth!" It startled me. He sounded exactly like Jack Nicholson from the movie *A Few Good Men*. Funnier still was the fact that I understood every word the guy said.

I asked Rick why the guy had said that. Rick replied that the two of them had been discussing the movie. Chuckling, I mentioned that, for the first time that night, I finally understood something the guy had said. Rick laughed then told the guy what I had said. The guy looked back at me and smiled.

"If you want," he said, sporting the Jack Nicholson accent. "I can speak this way from now on."

I agreed and from there we started talking. He held on to the accent the entire time. It's the closest I've ever come to talking with a celebrity. I've got to say, it was a blast.

Now on to my mom. We were on the same trip to Prague that I chronicled earlier. One thing that I didn't mention is that Mom broke her wrist right before her trip to visit us overseas. And she was miserable. She held a brave face but every bump on the road made her wince. Whenever we were on a street car or train she had to sit down right away. Staying on her feet not only hurt, but it was hard to hang on to a pole with only one usable hand.

After a long day of exploring Prague, we were ready to head back to our guesthouse outside the city. Like always, we took the commuter train. It was full with no place for Mom to sit. Finally, the train stopped and a man got off. Mom honed in on the empty seat he left behind. So did another woman, but Mom was faster. She bolted toward the seat and got it first. Victory!

Everyone around us gave my mom a strange look. We had no idea why. Then the train stopped again. Another man got off but no one in the car went for his empty seat. Slowly and unsurely, the poor woman Mom had bested earlier hobbled over to the space. We realized right away she was terribly handicapped, her legs bowing like she'd just ridden a horse at eight feet wide.

Oops. Ugly Americans are we. We bowed our heads in shame the rest of the way back.

Finally, the tale of naked Gerard Depardieu. Okay, I'm not really sure it was him. But it looked like the guy and, given the peeing incident a little while ago, there's a ~~slim~~ great chance it was him.

Rick and I were in Paris taking a night-time cruise along the Seine River. We had befriended a couple of women who were visiting from Miami. It was fun pointing out things together, "Hey, look! The Eiffel Tower and the Louvre. What is that? A mini Statue of Liberty?" Then we came upon the Notre Dame cathedral, the famous church with flying buttresses and limping hunchbacks.

At that point, the river ran like a canal between two stone walls. The streets of Paris were twenty feet up. Near water's edge there was a lower embankment a few feet wide where people seemed to enjoy hanging out. On the night in question one of those people included a man without a single stitch of clothing on him. He looked just like the famed actor as he strolled along, seemingly without a care as we gawked at him from the boat. The captain of the vessel shined a spot light on him. Looking at us, he looked mildly surprised, as if thinking, "Oh. Where did that boat come from? Huh." He must have missed the five other tour boats in front of us. Come on. It was tourist season.

As we chuckled, one of our new friends whipped out her camera and focused the lens on him. Click. She took a photo. Not thinking, I said, "Ew! I can't believe you took a picture of him!"

She replied, "Why not? I don't see things like that every day. Do you?"

I couldn't say that I did, nor could I say I ever wanted to see it ever again. Still, I must say it was pretty funny and, honestly, I'd kill to see that photo now, though probably just from the waist up.

# ViOLeNT aCT of RaNDoMNeSS!

### *Dear Make-Believe Mom #2* -- August 4, 2010

**Dear Mom,**
I'm totally in love with this really great guy. He is everything I want and he says the same about me. So what's the problem? I met him on the internet. I really want to meet him in person and he wants to meet me, too, but he insists on doing it in an out-of-the-way place without anyone else around. He's said it'll be more romantic that way, but I'm a little nervous. What should I do? - **In Heaven on the Internet Highway**

**Dear Heaven,**
First of all, congratulations! Second of all, *RUN!* This guy is totally bad news.

I'm not saying this because you met him on the internet. After all, only 99.9% of guys you meet there are serial rapists and/or killers. There's always that .01%. But trust me, if he's really that awesome and thinks you two are meant to be, he should have NO problem meeting you in a controlled environment WITH YOUR PARENTS PRESENT. If he makes excuses like "I'm afraid your folks won't like me, and if I lose you…" or "I want our first meeting to be special, I can meet them next time" then drop him like a hot tamale. Other danger words? "No one understands me like you." No-one = his parole officer, wife or state-appointed psychiatrist. There's also "We have a forbidden love. People just won't understand 'us.'" He means local, state, or federal judges.

Now if he buckles and says he'll meet you with your parents at your house, don't take the bait. He just wants your home address. If you give it to him, he'll more than likely find his way there when your parents are conveniently absent. And that would be bad, very bad.

Trust me on this. I've seen and heard too many bad things on the news already. Don't be a statistic. Be smart.

**Dear Mom,**
My mom started this website/blog for teen girls and it is totally ridiculous. She's constantly saying stupid things and giving stupid advice and everyone knows it's MY MOM. Why in the world is she doing this? Does she really think she's that cool? Talk about delusional. Personally, I think she's just trying to embarrass me. Tell me, what should I do? - **Mad at my Mom**

**Dear Mad,**
Now, now. I'm sure everyone has been embarrassed by their parents at some point in their life. I know I have. But I've got to be honest with you – your mom sounds like one hip n' happenin' lady. If I were you, I'd be proud. And trust me, if she really wanted to embarrass you, creating a website would be the last thing she'd do. She'd probably just post an old picture of you passed out on the couch after a late-night Carnation Instant Formula binge. Now THAT would be embarrassing.

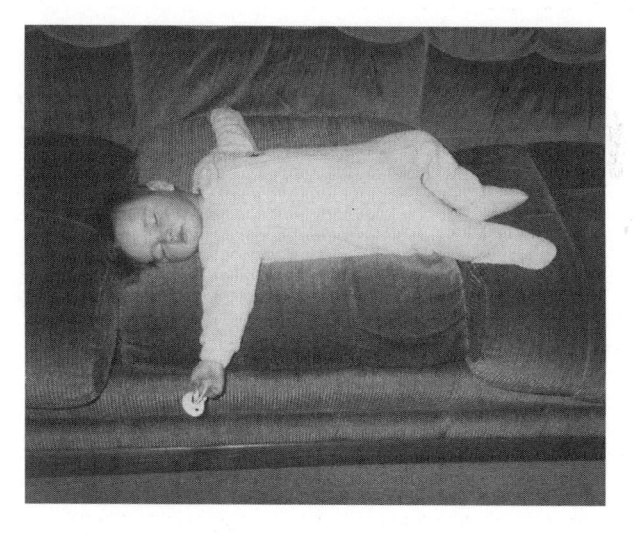

My advice? Suck it up and see your mother for the truly awesome person she is. Make sure to tell her so.

## CHAPTER 7
## If You Are What You Wear, I'm Sunk

Growing up I had a love/hate relationship with clothes. I loved them but hated never having enough money to buy all that I needed. For those of you who mock me, saying I didn't "need" those clothes I just "wanted" them, I can't respond. They clearly do not understand.

From a young age -- long before I cracked open a fashion magazine -- I felt my clothes defined me, which sucked because my mom didn't feel the same way. Somehow she felt the money should be better spent on less important things, like food and car repairs. For years I was forced to wear the all-time worst badge of fashion shame: Sears' Tough Skins. Coming in a wide variety of colors and patterns (yes, I said *patterns*), they were jeans "so rugged we [Sears] made a trampoline out of them!" Oh, the humiliation.

*No one in our family escaped.*

Finally, when I was in the sixth grade, the fashion gods shined their light into my dark world of style despair. A specialty clothing store opened up in our local mall. It had clothes for super neato kids like me. The name of the chic boutique was The Children's Place. That's right, fashion mecca. I begged my mom to take me there. I was *twelve*, for goodness's sake. It was time for some real duds. Girls had already started dividing themselves between the fashion haves and have-nots. I couldn't be left behind.

My mom relented, at last understanding the importance of fashionable clothes. With a sigh, she hustled me, my sister and brother into the car and headed to the mall.

I still remember the tremor of excitement I felt when I entered The Children's Place. All the awesome clothes! Electric blue satin jackets with pants to match, baseball jerseys... OMG! They had straight leg jeans instead of bell bottoms! So. Fashion. Forward.

This store obviously had all the latest trends. Whatever clothes I scored, I knew my classmates would be jealous. Still, I couldn't go nuts. Mom was the one with the checkbook. I had to choose my items carefully. And I did. I found the perfect outfit, one that would instantly classify me as cool. Grabbing it off the rack, I ran to the changing room and tried it on.

It was a pine green corduroy A-line skirt with western-inspired matching vest. I paired it with a white, orange and green plaid shirt. I still remember the goofy vibrato in my voice when I yelled to my mom, "This is it, Mom. I found my outfit!"

I must have said that a little too loudly because Mom hushed me right away. "For god's sake, Janene, they're just clothes."

But they weren't just clothes. They were my ticket to acceptance.

*I'm going to be a cool kid now,* I thought as I strutted out of the changing room. If Ralph Lauren had seen me as I walked toward the three-way mirror, he'd have signed me up to be his model. In front of the mirror, I struck one glamorous pose after another. My mom approved -- or maybe she was just tired of watching me act like a fool. Either way, she bought the outfit.

*Here it is! My glasses only added to my awesomeness.*

That wasn't the end, though. I still had one more item on my list and it was crucial. "I need some jeans, Mom. The real kind. Not Tough Skins."

Realizing she couldn't put if off anymore, Mom sighed and took me to The Gap.

The Gap was the only place where you could get the coolest jeans known to man. I'm talking Levi's, of course. Those new designer jeans like Gloria Vanderbilt and Jordache? I surmised that trend wouldn't last long. I mean, Levi's. LEVI'S! Everybody had them and it was time I had them, too. The spirit of all that is good and in vogue must have been whispering into my mom's ears because she bought me two pairs.

Later that night, I had to choose what to wear to school the next day. The green corduroy sensation or the Levi's? I went with the Levi's. I couldn't blow kids away with my new fashion sense so fast. I had to ease into my new identity.

The following day, as I walked around in the school in my new jeans, I felt like I was walking on a collar poppin' cloud. I was stylin' and profilin', as well as a bunch of other verbs ending with "in'." I was cool.

My new life as a fashion maven was great for the first few classes of school. Then right around fifth period, I went to the water fountain for a drink. My school nemesis was there. He looked me up and down and smirked. "So you think you're so cool now that you finally joined the real world and got a decent pair of jeans?"

If my ego were a bubble, all I can say is "Pop!" My stupid nemesis and his razor-sharp deductions! Still, it proved to me that kids did pay attention to what I was wearing. It mattered. And that hunch that designer jeans would go in and out of style fast? I'm glad I didn't bet the farm on that one. Designer jeans got HUGE.

### SHIELDED FROM SOCIETY

I still remember crying to my parents back in 1981. Desperate, I begged for a pair of Calvin Klein jeans. They said absolutely not. Why? Full blame can be placed on fifteen year-old super model, Brooke Shields.

"Look at the Calvin Klein ad on TV next time it comes on," my parents said.

I did. There sat Brooke, legs spread in those awesome jeans, whistling away. After she finished using those pouty lips to perform a stirring rendition of My Darling Clementine, she looked into the camera and said, all sexy-like, "Wanna know what comes between me and my Calvins? Nothing."

Wait. Huh? She wasn't wearing underwear? How uncomfortable. Not to mention...

Holy guacamole --Brooke Shields was a skank!

Okay, so maybe she was just the victim of pedophiles who claimed they were advertising executives. It didn't matter. I didn't get those jeans. At least I wasn't the only girl who didn't. It seems using fifteen year-old girls claiming they didn't wear underwear was not the best marketing strategy. Surprise.

Over the years, there have been many fashion items and trends. Some were awesome, others not so much. One of my first posts dealt with one of the not-so-great ones that, as of this writing, still seems to be going strong: butt cracks. You heard me, butt cracks. Granted, it's not as bad as it once was. I used to see more crack on a daily basis than Dan the Drug Dealer. Even so, we are still subjected to wearing those low slung jeans that let it all hang out. And, yes, I said "we." Not only do I have to see a bunch of cute girls' cracks when I sit on the bleachers at a basketball game, I have to bear the humiliation of knowing my own -- much fatter -- butt might also be on display. Okay, okay. I know they make shirts longer these days. Most of the time things stay under wraps. But still, who among us can't admit to an accidental showing of butt cleavage? I dare say no one!

So why ARE we willing become slaves of fashion? I'm not the first to ask. The topic has been argued for years. But as the debate goes on, so does our apparent willingness to take whatever *Vogue* prescribes.

So at this point you may be wondering, what did moms wear back in the day that she'd rather not admit to now? Many might not tell you but I will. Cue the wavy lines on the screen as I flashback to my younger days...

*Ahhh...those pants. Those wonderful, wonderful pants. They were light blue, with silhouettes of pink, purple and navy ponies all over them. Dare I say they were groovy? I was only eight or so, but my love affair with fashion began when I got those pants. I realized how my clothing could express my identity, how what I wore announced to the world who I was. Now why I felt a pair of pony pants accomplished that is something I'll reserve for a therapist, but I will tell you that when I wore them I felt fabulous. I* **was** *fabulous...*

Oops! Sorry that was just me. I promised you some dirt on all of today's moms. Are you ready? Here it is: knickers. No, I don't mean the British term for undies. I mean those ridiculous cut-at-the-knee poofy pants that Thomas Jefferson wore while writing the Declaration of Independence. Well in the early 80s they made a minor comeback. Did I think they looked weird? Yes. Did I buy a pair? Of course! Who was I to question the fashion industry? Now here's the really interesting part: when I searched for a stock photo of someone wearing a pair, I couldn't find one. Not one! Smelling a conspiracy, I hunkered down and finally found some carefully hidden evidence to back my claim. Exhibit A: a Vintage 1980s McCalls Knickers Sewing Pattern. And they thought they could shield you from past horrors. Ha!

Luckily, the fad didn't last long and, let's face it, not all moms are the same age as me. Many may not have worn them. But there were other, equally goofy trends to which they might have fallen victim. Like the time we all wore our over-sized sweatshirts inside out, or delved into neon. (I nearly burned out my eyeballs with that one.) We also had the Preppy phase with everyone running around in polo shirts, wide wale corduroys and sweaters tied around their necks like Superman capes. Ugh. Plus there was the *Flashdance* craze (more on that later) and the whole Madonna thing, too. (Anyone need a pair of lace gloves cut off at the fingers? I didn't think so. )

Trust me, there's plenty for moms to be embarrassed about, and I haven't even talked about Eighties hair yet. So if your mom ever gives you a goofy look when you debut the latest trend, I've got just the right ammunition. Just say, "Hey, mom? How many pairs of legwarmers did you own?" I guarantee she'll pass judgment no more. That is, unless your butt crack is showing.

No more butt cracks... *please!*

### THE HORROR...*THE HORROR!*

You know, one thing you learn as you get older is that fashion is like a girl with a limited wardrobe: it repeats. It may take decades and might not be exactly the same but, but like Arnold Schwarzenegger's Terminator, trends always come back. In fact fashion historian James Laver (1899- 1975) created a timeline to explain the general attitude of a particular fashion style. Called Laver's Law, it goes like this:

> 10 years before: indecent
> 5 years before: shameless
> 1 year before: daring
> "current fashion": smart
> 1 year after: dowdy
> 10 years after: hideous
> 20 years after: ridiculous
> 30 years after: amusing
> 50 years after: quaint
> 70 years after: charming
> 100 years after: romantic
> 150 years after: beautiful

Though Laver's Law was created in 1937, I think it still holds pretty true today. Perhaps that's why I cringed when the still ridiculous/not quite amusing item called "jeggings" re-emerged on the fashion scene during the fall of 2010. As a nation, we'd been down a similar road before and it ended in tragedy. I must admit, as of this writing we've still managed to avoid a fashion apocalypse.

But it's only a matter of time. Beware...BEWARE!

If you're not familiar with jeggings, they're a jean/leggings combo that can be worn in lieu of pants. Stylish, huh? I would LOVE to find out who designed these super sassy things so I can *hunt them down and burn them at the stake.*

You heard me. I am not pleased. Don't get me wrong, I know they didn't have me in mind when they created them. No one, and I mean *no one*, wants to see my thunder thighs sporting a pair. Jeggings were created for the typical American teenager. You know, the 5'10", 100 lb. girl with big boobs, tiny waist and long, lean legs? She's featured in all the magazines... Oh, sorry. Most girls don't look like that? Well just whip out the lip gloss and mark a big 'ole "L" in the middle of their foreheads right now.

Anyway, just because the target market for these cool puppies is limited to the perfectly proportioned, don't think others won't wear them. Because they will, my dears. THEY WILL. And I'm not talking about total infiltration of high schools or colleges. Young girls have much prettier bodies than their fragile self-esteem allows them to believe. And I'm not talking about people who are fit, those who work out or refrain from eating butter on a stick.

There are other people out there, people who latch onto fashion trends despite their ability to wear them. These individuals must be protected from themselves or we, as a nation, will face an ocular doom of ungodly magnitude.

So begins my cautionary tale....

Others may remember it differently, but for me things really started taking shape in 1983 with the movie *Flashdance,* a sweet tale starring Jennifer Beals about a beautiful welder/exotic dancer who dreamed of performing for a real ballet company. You should have seen her. She was a maniac, maniac on the floor! She was dancing like she'd never danced before! Then she dumped a bucket of water on herself and the crowd went wild.

But I digress. The important thing is what the dancers wore: leotards, leggings, and leg warmers. (Oh, man. A chill just went down my spine when I wrote 'leg warmers.') In addition to all that, there was Jennifer's signature piece, the over-sized sweatshirt. Anyway, after the movie came out everyone wanted to have "the look."

Now thanks to a national aerobics craze fueled by Jane "Make it Burn" Fonda's illustrious videos, leggings (and legwarmers) had already worked their way into the gym. Once *Flashdance* debuted and girls saw super stylish young women wearing them instead of just super old (yet admittedly buff) ones, leggings started popping up everywhere. They officially became cool.

In the beginning, people wore them with the signature sweatshirts. Then they moved on to tunics. Oh! I'd be remiss to omit Madonna's huge influence, too. She made the leggings/skirt combo very chic. As time moved on, big wide belts were added to the mix, fashionably cinched at the waist.

For many years leggings were incorporated into a number of looks, all reflections of the times. They all had one thing in common, though: one's butt was ALWAYS covered.

Then one day tragedy struck.

Quicker than Jimmy Dean could say "sausage links," a horrifying practice emerged that left many fashion victims in its wake. People started thinking – no, dare I say *believing* – that leggings could be worn as plain old pants. I can't remember the exact year when it happened (sorry, I'm still dazed from the experience) but one fair morning in the early Nineties we woke up to discover the cute leggings trend had suddenly transformed to something more like this:

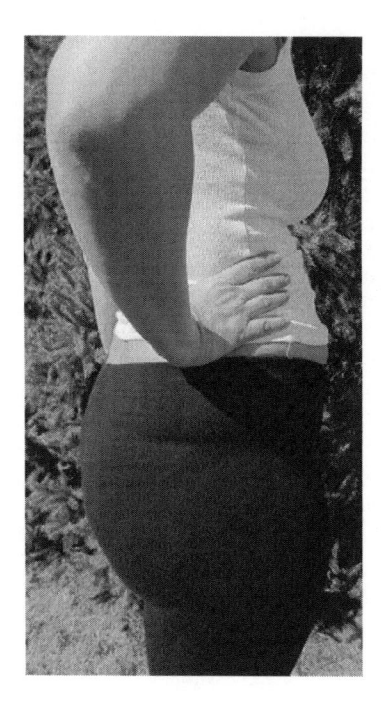

Frankly, that's more than I needed to see.

And now it's happening again. Leggings already made their mild comeback, our first cause of alarm. Plus watching jeans go from flared to skinny? Buttock-challenged females are still in a state of shock. And now we have jeggings. I ask you, do we really need to see and/or reveal every pucker and bulge again? I, for one, do not. Still, there will be those who blindly indulge, ending in results that will horrify.

So what do we do? Scorn the poor, unknowing fashion victims? No. Our wrath must be targeted at the real criminals: the lame-brained designers who brought jeggings to life. I mean, come on. We all come in different shapes and sizes. Why force an item which only 11.3% of the population looks good in? I know their job is to make us feel physically inadequate, but this is taking it way too far.

I, for one, am standing up to this injustice. I hope you will join me, too. Do everyone a favor: say no to jeggings. Trust me, the world will thank you.

### PUTTING YOUR BEST FOOT FORWARD

Of course, there are trends so inventive and ground-breaking that no one has ever seen them before. Guys wearing jeans below their butts? That was a first and, I hope, a last. I must admit, I don't get every trend and style that has entered the recent fashion scene. Part of it is because I'm older, but it's mostly because the trends are stupid, so unlike the cool trends we had while I was growing up. Those rainbow suspenders made cool by Mork from TV's *Mork and Mindy*? That was high fashion, folks. And shoulder pads so massive they could be used as flotation devices? Totally chic.

Seriously, sometimes I wonder what the fashion world is thinking. I wonder what we're thinking, too. We're buying this stuff, so we can't blame it all on the designers. Case in point: something I saw a couple years ago. I must say there is nothing more disturbing than witnessing a footwear atrocity first-hand. Okay, that's not true but let's pretend. Here are the facts:

A year ago, I found myself in the Kohl's shoe department. I say "found" because I can't remember why I was there and, trust me, when I go to Kohl's for footwear there is always a reason. The back clearance room in Von Maur? That trip is pure recreation. When I go to Kohl's for shoes, I go with a purpose. That's just the way I roll.

Anyway, I'm in the Kohl's shoe department and I see them: a

certain style of sandal (extra points for alliteration) that had been unleashed on the world last year. They were ridiculous. I thought they would be in and out of fashion in less than a hummingbird heartbeat. Yet, here they were for season two and they had multiplied. A full row of different variations was dedicated to this style. That's part one.

Part two happened a few days later. I was back in Kohl's shoe department due to a shoe emergency that has no bearing on this story. Plus it might make one of my family members mad so my lips are sealed. Anyway, remembering the row of ridiculous sandals I brought my camera, thinking it would be fun to take a picture of it and write a post. Well, guess what. Only one style still remained on the display shelf. Below it looked like this:

That's right. Only two boxes remained.
From that photo, I'm not sure if you can appreciate the full glory

of this sandal so here's a close up:

Seriously? What was I not seeing? Was there some chilly ankle epidemic I wasn't aware of? A sudden fancy for cankles? I couldn't remember the last summer day when I said, "My toes are so hot but my ankles are so cold! Why don't they have sandals for that?"

Maybe I was just out of touch, but those things looked incredibly silly. To my chagrin, the whole cankle look is still in vogue. I guess the hot toes/cold ankle concern is valid. What do I know anyway? I'm sitting here in a black hoodie with a glow-in-the-dark Batman symbol emblazoned across the chest. Which is AWESOME.

Anyway, I'm not finished with the whole fashion/appearance thing. I've only identified the issue. Before we move on I think it wise that we revisit the more salient points of our discussion:

1. For a long time, I felt that clothes defined a person.

2. Evidence acquired in my young life supported that theory.

3. There have been many stupid fashion trends over the years, *ergo...*

4. By definition, we are all morons.

But let's get back to the most important topic at hand: me. My clothing tales of woe aren't over. Let me take you to the highest of highs and the lowest of lows in my fashion journal.

### A GROWTH EXPERIENCE

It was two weeks before my freshman year of high school and I was giddy with excitement. For years my mom had promised me a whole new wardrobe when I got to high school. Cha-ching! I was finally cashing in.

There were no siblings this time. It was just her, me, and her wallet. We made quite a trio. We went from shop to shop and bought the coolest stuff. The grand total: $300. Even by today's standards that's a decent chunk of change. But back in 1980, it was the equivalent of $240,000. More or less. Like I may have said before, math isn't my strongest subject.

Now we weren't fools. Only a few items could be worn during the hot first few weeks of school. We went for longevity. We wanted to make sure I looked stunning every season of the year. We bought sweaters, wide-whale corduroy pants, long-sleeve shirts and a gorgeous beige corduroy blazer. I couldn't wait for winter to come so I could wear them. Everyone would be so jealous!

Well, I never got to wear them. Why? Because over the next six weeks I grew three inches taller. Nothing fit and nothing could be taken back. There they hung in my closet, tags still on. I cried. My mom cried harder. I suspect my dad, Mr. Iron Wallet, shed a few tears of his own.

As you may have guessed, my freshman year in high school didn't end up becoming my best fashion year. My clothing budget had been blasted to oblivion. There was no money for new clothes. No, my mom didn't make me go to school naked. I got a few pairs of jeans, some shirts, and a new winter coat.

I also got a job. Okay, I already had one. You see, my dad had his own business. Oftentimes he worked weekends. I started to work them, too. Slaving in the bindery department of his printing company, I collated paper for cash. Was it fun? Heck no. It sucked. But it allowed me to buy the clothes that I *needed*.

That's when I got smart. My clothing dollars no longer came from my folks. It was *my* hard-earned cash being spent. It could not be wasted. I organized my clothing, figured out what I *really* needed. I shopped for deals. From that day on, I found myself unable to buy things at full retail price. That's still holds true today.

### WEARING ME DOWN

Here's the thing, though. As much as I loved fashion, some of the styles that emerged seemed...well, not my style. You know the phrase "you are what you wear"? I began to question its validity. It all started during my last year in college. I was in a business class. We were discussing job interviews. During the discussion, one of the students raised his hand and said, "It's not fair. I've got great grades and I'm a hard worker, but as soon as I walk into an interview I know I don't have a shot, all because of my hair."

He was right. Why? Because he had Jon Bon Jovi hair. No, not the cool stylings of the present day Bon Jovi. This was the Eighties, people. Imagine a teased out poodle with twenty-inch long hair extensions exploding from its head.

Now a lot of girls thought Bon Jovi's hair was totally rad back then, but job interviewers? Different story. The teacher looked at the guy and said, "Why don't you just cut your hair?"

The student replied, "Because it's me. Why can't people just look past it to see the kind of guy I am?"

Then the teacher said, *"If people have to look past your hair to see the real you, then maybe your hair really isn't 'you.'"*

Interesting point.

Long story short: the kid cut his hair and landed a job soon afterward. Ain't it sweet when things wrap up so easily?

You know, we keep being told you can't judge a book by its cover. Still, we do it all the time. Why? Maybe because we *can* make certain judgments based on one's appearance. After all, the way people dress reflects who they are, right? Just go through any high school in the U.S. and it's not too tough to point out the jocks, goths, preps, nerds and stoners pretty easily. As for the Eighties? I've got to tell you, even back then a guy with Bon Jovi hair would not have been pegged as a smart, hard working Business major. Looks like this case is closed.

*However...*

Though sometimes the way people dress reflects who they are, sometimes it just doesn't. Some people hide behind their clothes as if they were wearing a mask. Others feel pressure to blend in and wear clothes for approval. Others just wear what's hanging in the closet without care for what message they're sending.

Isn't it funny how what one person feels totally comfortable wearing can make someone else feel totally *un*comfortable? I still remember when Laura Ashley dresses were popular in the Eighties. These floral print sack dresses had long, gathered skirts, puffy sleeves, and a price tag that made even the richest of teen girls weep. Still, they bought them, wearing them with hair bows, pearls, and -- here's the really embarrassing part -- bobby socks and Keds. The look was hot. The look was cool. This meant, of course, I bought one, too.

When I wore it I felt like a moron.

Not that I didn't look good. The dress was beautiful and I had all the proper accessories. But it wasn't me. What many considered comfortable, I considered a costume. Even though I blended in, I felt like I stood out.

But back to the whole job thing. Let's say there are two girls. One is wearing sweats, gym shoes, and the whole ponytail-with-a-rubber-band-around-the-head thing. Another is wearing a black leather jacket, matching lipstick, and a nose ring. If I needed someone to help me with an after school fitness program for kids, who do you think I'd hire first? For all I know, the goth chick is an awesome athlete and great with kids, but she surely didn't dress for the part.

If you want a certain job you've got to dress for it. That's always been the case. We don't see a lot of accountants running around in kimonos and bamboo flip flops, do we? Still, what about that lone accountant who really wants to wear one? What if wearing a kimono reflects who he or she really is?

I don't know if I have any real answers here. I just know if you want to be taken seriously, you've got to dress that way. When it comes to work -- heck, when it comes to *life* -- sometimes you're required to wear a costume. It sucks but it's true.

So judging a book by its cover? We have to recognize that people do it every day. As for how we use this information, that's up to the individual. I won't be one to judge. ;)

Of course, when I became a new mom all of this fashion business was crammed down a Diaper Genie. Having babies broke me as well as my wallet. It wasn't pretty. There was no money for new clothes. We needed other things, like baby food and Tickle Me Elmos. As for the nice clothes I had? They were moth-balled to protect them from projectile poop and vomit.

The kids are older now and I'm back to my fashion ways, though my budget is still slashed. Unfortunately, one of the duties of being a parent is clothing your kids. So while I spend the same amount of money on clothes, only a fraction goes towards me.

It wouldn't be so bad if my kids actually cared about clothes. They don't -- at least not all of them. My oldest -- who is also my only daughter -- could give a flying Ferragamo as to what she wears. Had I not been right there when I gave birth to her, I would swear she wasn't my daughter. As for my oldest son, he's even worse. He puts his shirts on backwards just to make me mad. My youngest son, though? It appears he's acquired a smidgeon of my style gene.

I still remember a few years ago when he was eight years-old. I'd just come home from doing damage with a Kohl's thirty percent off coupon. Bringing the gray bag up to his room, I pulled out tons of new pants and shirts to supplement his wardrobe. After I showed him the loot, he shook his head in exasperation. Then he looked right into my eyes and said, "I can't wear any of this. It's like you don't even know me, Mom."

Sigh.

## ViOLeNT aCT of RaNDoMNeSS!
### ACTION FIGURE JESUS

If you're familiar with my blog then you may know about my buddy, Action Figure Jesus. I came upon him during my travels to Seattle, Washington. I have to say, he's quite an inspiration. I still remember when I brought him home. It was our first day back from the trip and we were starving. I'd yet to go to the store and had nothing to feed my brood. Enter Action Figure Jesus:

Boy, he really helped us that day. There were grilled cheese sandwiches for all! From that day forward, Action Figure Jesus took a place of prominence on my desk.

Well, just today I was taking some photos for my blog and the batteries in my camera died. I had no others in the house. Argh! What was I to do? The situation was dire. Very dire. I feared all was lost.

Now to fully illustrate the miracle you are about to witness, I must prove just how dire things were. See that poor little battery's lifeless body in the battery tester? I know. It brings tears to the eyes:

But wait! Who did I see but Action Figure Jesus coming to the rescue, once again. With a raise of his arms he raised my batteries from the dead. Another miracle!

My tears turned joyful when I popped the little guys back in the tester. Both batteries were once again full of life. Thank you, Action Figure Jesus!

# CHAPTER 8
# Bringing Home the Bacon

For those of you who say love makes the world go round, all I have to say is this: In 2012, Americans spent $17.6 billion on St. Valentine's Day. So while I'd choose love over money every time, I'd sure rather have them both. Having cash in your pocket makes life a little easier to love.

I remember the first time I purchased something. It was a gumball out of a machine. My three year-old fingers slid that penny in the slot, I turned the crank and then -- voila! Only the gumball wasn't purple like I'd hoped. A yellow one had popped out, instead. When I asked my mom for another penny, she just looked at me and said, "But you've already got a gumball." I replied, "But I wanted purple." With Forrest Gump-like wisdom, she replied, "When it comes to gumball machines, you get what you get. They all taste the same anyway. Just pretend yours is purple when you put it in your mouth."

What could I do? Purple gumballs tasted way better than yellow, but I had no money of my own. Sighing, I did my best to feel thankful for the gumball that I'd gotten but, you know...yellow.

Early on I realized I had to earn my own dough if I wanted to get the things I liked. Unfortunately, child labor laws restricted my money-making opportunities. Aside from scavenging underneath the couch cushions for the loose change that may or may not have trickled out of my dad's pants, I was sunk. Still, the lack of funds made me appreciate the value of money. When a spare quarter landed in my hot, little hands I treated it like gold. I was King Midas, Mini Me edition.

Money. Why do we love it so much -- outside of the fact that it can buy us almost anything? It can also cause so many headaches no matter how rich or poor we are. Some people say money doesn't matter. In many cases that happens to be true. But in others, it matters quite a bit. The big question is, when does it matter to you?

Everyone's relationship with money is different. My three kids serve as perfect examples. Each of them handles money differently. Still, they all usually have the same goal. They *all* want something. Yet, two of my kids are savers. The other one's a spender, through and through. In fact, if he were down to his last quarter and saw a gumball machine, he'd be flat busted broke before you could say "Rain-Blo." (*Editing note: during the process of re-reading this, I realized something profound about myself as a writer. I overuse gumball analogies. Now that I've recognized it I will stop.*)

Anyway, I'm different from most folks in that I don't mind having kids who constantly want things. Truth be told, I kind of like it. A kid who wants something requiring money is the first to clean the bathroom for a buck. What I can't stand are kids who want something for nothing. They have to be willing to work for it. I'm a nice person, but why should I have to shell out my own dough to feed someone else's iTunes obsession?

Sure, my kids get birthday and Christmas presents. New school clothes? Not a problem. They get special treats on other occasions, but many of their wants go unmet. That is, of course, unless they buy it themselves. Gotta love that motivation. There's nothing like seeing your kid work hard to earn something they want.

A bit ago, one of my savers finally salted away enough money to buy something they'd really wanted. I won't say how much it was. Just know it took them over a year, so we're talking major bucks. Would *I* have spent that much for the item in question? Honestly, no I wouldn't have. But it wasn't my money. They had earned it themselves. They had the right to spend it.

I guess what I'm saying is, in my book, you're not greedy if you really want something you don't need -- even if it's expensive. Just make sure you're willing to do the work to get it, and make sure you're willing to do without the other things that the same money could buy.

Take one of my kids. He'd give his eye teeth to make some cash. Literally. A while back I took him to the dentist for a checkup and the dentist found a problem. His adult eye teeth were growing in funny because the baby teeth they were replacing would not budge. "We're going to have to extract them," the dentist told me. *Extract* them? I asked the question that runs through every concerned mom's mind, "How much will that cost?" The dentist said, after insurance, it would cost fifty dollars a tooth. One hundred bucks!

Overhearing the conversation, my son proposed a deal. If he was able to wiggle the teeth out on his own, I would give him forty dollars. The price was steep, but I agreed. The proposal would still save me sixty dollars. Plus those teeth weren't loose at all. I wasn't sure he could do it. The extraction appointment was only two weeks away.

Well, the very next day my kid came home from school and handed me an envelope. A *bloody* envelope. Inside were two yanked out teeth. Gross.

"Oh my," I said. "How did you get them out so fast? Didn't it hurt?"

"Heck, yeah, it hurt, Mom. No pain, no gain." He held out his hand. "Forty dollars, please."

### MOM'S MONEY TIPS

These days it seems that people want the gain without the pain. Not only that, they want the gain *right now*. Unfortunately, there are more than a few businesses all too eager to accommodate them. These businesses have no problem giving people what they want right away at little cost...in the beginning. What people don't realize until too late is that the longer you wait to pay for something, the more expensive it becomes.

But never fear. I'm about to share some sage money advice with you. Not only that, it comes from one of the world's greatest financial minds: mine. ;) Warning: this advice is serious. When it comes to money, I don't joke around. But I'll start with a joke. Wanna hear it? Okay.

I'M FILTHY STINKIN' RICH!

Actually, it's not a joke. It's true because I found not one or two, but *three* separate credit card offers in my mailbox today. If I play things right, my spending power is about to increase three-fold! A world of riches will be mine, and the excitement doesn't even end there. The credit company I do use just sent me an updated card as well. Along with it they sent me another *completely different* card. I didn't have to ask!

That's right. I got an unsolicited American Express card. I thought it had to be a mistake. I'd never applied or even asked for one, but my credit card confirmed it was mine. You see, my credit card company had been worried because my current card wasn't accepted at Neiman Marcus. Oh, no! That's one of the very best places to get upscale, over-priced clothes. That's my kind of shopping... except it isn't, really. In fact, I only have one thing in my closet from Neiman Marcus: a Marc Jacobs black fringed top I'd found double tagged on a clearance rack at Filene's Basement.

Truth is, financially my family does okay because I *don't* go crazy with our credit cards. Cards can lure you into spending money, especially when you shouldn't. I still remember back during my college days when a friend got her very first card. Her first bill was $34. She let it slide, rolling the bill to next month. Then she rolled it again. Six months later, finance charges and late fees turned that $34 into over $200. She nearly had a heart attack.

When it comes to credit cards, don't carry too many and do your best to pay them off every month. My rule is if I can't pay for something straight out of my checking account, I can't afford it on my credit card bill, either.

If you want a few more tips when it comes to credit cards, loans and money, take a peek below:

**1. "Special offers" aren't really special.** If a company or salesman says you've been 'specially selected,' don't feel flattered. They just want your money. It's called marketing.

**2. "Low, easy payments" are no deal.** The lower your monthly payment, the more you pay in the end. Here's an example:

Say you take out a 6% loan for $5000.

- If you get a 1 year loan, you'll pay $430/month for 12 months. **TOTAL: $5164**.

- If you get a 3 year loan, you'll pay $152/month for 36 months. **TOTAL: $5476**.

- If you get a 5 year loan, you'll pay $97/month for 60 months. **TOTAL: $5800**.

**3. Always ask yourself: Do you need it now or can you wait?** If you can wait, put that money in the bank until you've saved enough to buy it outright. For all you know, by that time you might not need or want it anymore.

**4. Paying full retail price is for chumps.** Wait until it's on sale.

**5. Cars are an expense, not an investment.** Man, I've seen a lot of people become slaves to their car payments. Don't let that be you. Make sure to buy a vehicle you can comfortably afford. Plus remember, its value decreases as soon as you drive it off the dealer's lot.

**6. It's all about give and take.** If you find something expensive that you absolutely must have, ask yourself what you're willing to give up in order to get it.

**7. The little things add up**. A $3 cup of Starbucks coffee every morning = $90/month. Yowsers.

**8. Time is money**. If you make $8/hr and wait until those killer $60 jeans go on sale for $40, you're not just saving $20 but 2-1/2 hours of work.

I feel so empty inside...

That's all I've got for now. Make me proud and spend your money wisely! And if you're wondering what happened to those offers and the American Express card, they're shredded in the trash.

You know, when it comes to acquiring financial wisdom, I think there are four basic stages people go through. It's my own personal theory based on something we can all relate to -- the ice cream truck. Here they are:

**Stage 1:** It's summertime. You're playing in the yard when suddenly the faint sound of "Turkey in the Straw" tickles your ears. SQUEE! The ice cream truck is coming! You run inside and beg your mom for some cash. She says, "It's so expensive. We've got popsicles in the fridge." But that's just not the same. It's the ice cream truck! It's full of magic and rainbows and tasty treats that can't be beat. If your mom says yes, you are over the moon. If she says no, you run up to your room. Where is that $5 Grandma sent you as a special treat? YOU HAVE TO HAVE THAT ICE CREAM! You will die if you don't. You're sure of it.

**Stage 2:** It's summertime, once again. You're hanging out in the yard when that magical sound is heard again. ICE CREAM! Running inside, you ask your mom for some cash. She says the same thing she's told you 1000 times before: "Those ice cream trucks are a rip off." Maybe you'll be able to convince her just this one time to give you money to buy some. But if she doesn't, you won't be spending your own money. Like she said, it's kind of a rip off.

**Stage 3:** Summer returns. You're lounging on the deck, texting your friends when you hear that fateful song. The ice cream truck. You wonder what Mom has stowed away in the freezer. An ice cream sandwich would taste great right about now.

**Stage 4**: Many years have passed and it's summertime again. You hear that god-forsaken tune in the distance. Bracing yourself, you hear your kids burst through the door and scramble your way. "The ice cream truck is coming! Can we have money?" they squeal. Oh, joyful rapture. The cost of one treat from that idiotic truck equals the price of a box of them at the store. Sigh. What to do, what to do...

## EDUCATION DEPRIVATION

If you really want to save a ton of money there is one other thing you must do -- don't have kids. Kidding! Actually, I'm only half kidding. Kids really do cost a lot. From diapers to dance lessons, it's amazing how much it costs to raise children these days. Of course, some things you just can't put a price tag on, like the joy of parenting. Sure, there are days when the word "joy" is substituted with "horror" but that topic has been covered already. What we haven't covered yet is the price of going to college. That's a frightening subject.

I'm still shaking in my boots after my daughter and I visited two colleges last fall. It's hard to believe that my little girl has grown up so fast. Even harder? That college costs have grown faster.

I shouldn't complain too much. The first college we saw was only $15,000 per year. That's a bargain considering what other colleges are charging. The second school costs $43,000 per year! It does have a great scholarship program. Still, the whole bill will cost well over $100,000K.

*This view is yours for an arm and a leg!*

Did you know the average cost of college has risen by nearly 600% from the time I went in 1985? That's three times faster than the consumer price index. What's worse, a lot of students are having trouble finding jobs after graduation. Oh, what wonderful news. I can't imagine the joy of leaving school without a job but with a HUGE student loan.

So why are so many kids still going to college? As a parent, my answer is because I'm scared. The gap between rich and poor is getting wider and I'm worried that my kids will be left behind. For all I know, in ten years you'll need a master's degree to serve a caramel macchiato at Starbucks. Plus the rate of unemployment for college grads is half the national average -- a fact not lost on me.

Of course, that's not the only reason. College also gives you that ever important factor called **prestige**. Also, you do learn a lot -- and not just academic stuff, but a lot of necessary life skills. You learn self-discipline and how to organize your time. You learn to take responsibility for your actions. You learn how to work with others -- both one on one and in groups -- as well as how to cook Ramen noodles. Plus you really learn the value of a dollar. I still remember when my grandma used to send me $5 in the mail. I'd float around all day, feeling like Donald Trump without the freaky hairstyle.

So no matter the cost, my kids are going to college. I'm sure it's a fact universities rely on. I just wish I could count on my kids not needing to live in my basement once they are done.

## PAY CHECK

It's tough how, these days, going to college no longer guarantees you'll get a good job when you're done. People have to be savvy when they choose a career. Simply put, when it comes to making money some jobs are definitely better than others. The phrase "do what you love and you'll never work a day in your life" is all well and good, but what if what you love to do comes with a salary that flat-out sucks? Is that okay with you? Can you give up that 60" LED TV for your dream job? There's no right or wrong answer here. It's a decision only you can make.

In college, I was a business major with a double major in marketing and management. During my last semester, I finally decided marketing research would be my career.

I called the biggest market research company in Chicago and talked to one of their recruiters. The phone conversation went well. I loved the details of the job and the company sounded great. Then we began to talk logistics -- getting me in for an interview, etc. I was incredibly eager until the interviewer said, "The starting salary for market research employees out of college is $13,500 per year."

Now this was 1989 and I know you understand the concept of inflation. In 1910, the average man made only $500 a year and his family did fine on that. So while a salary of $13,500 may sound horrific by today's standards -- particularly when living in Chicago (not cheap) -- in 1989 that amount of money was... still horrific.

"$13,500 a year? I'm not sure I could live on that," I told the recruiter.

He replied, "Just live with your parents for a few years. That's what most of our new people do."

It is said the average person changes careers five to seven times in their life. Well, I made my first change before I even left the gate. *Live with my parents?* It was one thing to live with them for a little while so I could build up some cash to buy a place. But live with them because I couldn't afford to pay rent on a studio apartment? No way. I'd made a third more money last summer working as a temporary employee!

Now had I loved market research, *dreamed* market research, it might have been worth it to me. But I didn't, so it wasn't. I decided to do a little market research of my own. I investigated all the different jobs in my field and figured out which ones appealed to me. Then I targeted the jobs inside that group that made a decent wage. That's when my real search began.

It took a while. I didn't get a job right out of college, but you've already heard that tale of woe. But I did have a clearer picture of what I wanted, and I'm not just talking about a job.

**COMPUTATION ERROR**

I don't want you to misunderstand me. Following your heart can be a beautiful thing. I know people who make good money but they're miserable because they hate their job. I also know a few folks who don't make much at all but simply love what they do. There are even a few who have both -- they love their jobs and they make a good wage. Huzzah! Take my brother. He ended up okay and he did it by...well, following his heart. I've got to say, when he was young I was worried he wouldn't end up in the position he is now.

Before I tell my brother's story, though, I've got to mention I owe him big. Why? Because he wasn't just the youngest kid in our family but he was also the only boy. That meant he was subjected to -- how can I say this politely? -- undue torture, girl style. As an example, my sister and I used to love treating him to full facials, make up and all. He was always a good sport. Of course, the day finally came when he said enough. I can't remember how old he was at the time. Maybe 19? 20? Anyway, that was one of many things we did to poor Jimmy. He put up with a lot.

I don't want to give you the wrong impression. Sometimes the torture went the other way. As the youngest, he employed many classic tactical maneuvers on my sister, Heather, and me. Take poking. Out of the blue, he'd come up to one of us and poke us in the ribs. We'd say, "Jimmy, cut that out." Then he'd do it again. "Jimmy, I said 'Cut that out!'" He'd still do it again. And again. Finally we would poke him back. Then he'd scream like a banshee engulfed in flames. My mom would hear him then yell as us. "Girls, leave your little brother alone! Jim, come here and I'll get you a cookie."

He was conniving, too. The one thing that riled Heather and me most is how he always seemed to get out of setting the dinner table. We took turns and whenever it was his time to do it he'd employ his Peanuts' teacher strategy. Don't know what that is? We didn't either. Here's a rundown of how it went:

Jim would be upstairs in his room on the computer while Heather and I were down in the family room watching *Brady Bunch* reruns on TV. The kitchen was right next to the family room, making us easy pawns in Jim's devious game. As Mom was getting dinner ready, she would call up the stairs, "Jim, it's your turn to set the table!" Jim would say something back. Mom would go, ""What?" and then Jim would say whatever he'd said before, only with more conviction. She'd say, "What?" again, and he'd reply the same way once more. Mom would go into the family room. Shaking her head in frustration, she'd say, "I don't know what you're brother is saying. One of you girls set the table tonight. I'll make sure he does it tomorrow."

Sometimes he did set the table the very next day. Most of the time, he didn't.

One day, Heather and I wised up. When it came close to dinner time we went up to our rooms. Sure enough, a few minutes later we heard Mom from the bottom of the stairs. "Jim, it's your turn to set the table!" And here's what our lovely brother said back:

"Hom imna cant I'msa bo limsha moreint."

"What?" Mom called up to him.

"HOM IMNA CANT I'MSA BO LIMSHA MOREINT!"

What? That was gibberish! No wonder she couldn't understand him! That little booger. Heather and I ran down to the kitchen to expose his deception.

"Mom!" we said, "Jim wasn't saying real words! He was speaking garbage to frustrate you so he could get out work!"

Mom just looked at us wearily and said, "Is that so? Well, while you're here, the two of you can set the table."

And that was Jim, or at least a part of Jim. There were and are a lot of great things about him. In fact, he ended up becoming one of the most incredibly hilarious people I know. Incredibly creative, too. But there was something about Jim in junior high that disturbed me a lot. Jim was one of those kids who was unbelievably talented, unbelievably creative, as well as unbelievably UNDER achieving.

Don't get me wrong, he was a good student but he clearly didn't have his heart in it. I shook my head at him all the time. It killed me to think of all the great things he could achieve it he'd only put his mind to it. But no. Instead of concentrating all his energy on school, he followed his heart and dove into a silly hobby. It revolved around this weird thing Mom and Dad had just bought. What was it called, again? Oh, yeah.

A personal computer.

My folks brought it home in 1981. I admit it was kind of neat. But all that Franklin Ace 1000 could really do was word-processing plus some basic spreadsheets.

Well, Jim thought that maybe the machine could do more. Ridiculous, I know. He spent hours on it, learning code on his own through trial and error. Well, guess what? Much to my surprise it turned he COULD teach the computer to do different things. Cool things.

As you may have guessed, Jim ended up doing all right in life. Did I tell you he works at Microsoft as an inventor? Not a bad gig for a guy who chose to follow his heart instead of the pre-programmed path for achievement. There might be a lesson in there somewhere.

*Me, my sis, Heather and Jim ...with a Frisbee on his head*

## KEEPING UP WITH THE JONESES

As you can see, there is more than one path to success, especially since success means different things to different people. For some it's all about the money. For others it's about happiness or the desire to make a difference. Some get lucky and get all three, which presents a dilemma in and of itself.

I'm sure you've heard the phrase "*keeping up with the Joneses.*" It's often used to describe the "act or making of purchases for status or image rather than out of need, especially for the purpose of competing with friends or neighbors." (Thank you, Wiktionary.) But did you ever wonder where it came from? Believe it or not, a comic strip.

Written by Arthur "Pop" Momand, the strip ran from 1916-1940 and was called – get this -- *Keeping Up with the Joneses*. Go figure! It featured the McGinises, a family living next to the "objects of envy," the Joneses. The Jones family had the best of everything. This, of course, translated into high social standing. Poor McGinises – they tried everything they could to keep up with the Joneses. Of course, they always failed.

And look where we are now, decades later. Folks are still trying. Why else would someone spend $300 on a Coach purse? For centuries, people have been judged by how much they make. And since people don't go around telling others what they earn, the only real way to judge wealth is by what they *spend*. Right?

Wrong.

Sure, a person living in a $500,000 house probably doesn't work at Burger King -- that is, unless they own it. At the same time, they might owe $475,000 on that house and struggle to make monthly payments. Across town you might have someone in a $250,000 home who owns it outright. Looks can be deceiving.

Still, there is that one family with TONS of dough. Remember that girl in your high school chemistry class? You know, the one who always talked about Spring Break in St. Thomas and how pissed she is that Daddy forgot to have seat warmers installed in her Mercedes. I bet *she* never had to beg for a pair of Lucky Jeans. No fair. If only you could have been her…

Well, guess what? Her life might have still sucked. Her parents might have fought all the time, or verbally abused her -- oh, man! They might have had an illegal slave trade business, forcing her to remain silent or be sold to a sultan in Kelantan! Or maybe…

Her life didn't suck. It might have been pretty cool. The injustice of it all!

I'd like to tell you that when you're older it doesn't matter, that people don't judge others by what they have, but I'd be lying. Many do. So what's my advice?

Fuhgettaboutit.

If you don't, it'll drive you crazy. There will ALWAYS be someone with more than you. Enjoy the things you have. And when you're finally in the workforce trying to earn a dime, remember this quote from a very wise and intelligent woman (a.k.a. me):

***"Some people make enough, some people don't, and it has nothing to do with their paycheck."***

Think on that for a minute. What kind of person do you want to be? Do you want to always need more, ever striving to keep up with the Joneses? Or will you choose to be content. It is a choice, you know.

Now I'm not giving you an excuse to be lazy. Ambition is a good thing. So are goals. Just make sure you're motivated for the right reasons. Also keep in mind that people who are never satisfied are, well, never satisfied. What fun is that? As for people who judge their self worth by the amount and/or quality of their possessions? That's just plain sad.

Okay, I'm done now. I hope you enjoyed that little ditty on trying to keep up with the Joneses. I've got to take a break now and get on Zappos so I can order these super cute Keens my friend just bought. They're probably more than I want to pay, but all the cool moms are wearing them and I don't want to look like a loser.

## ViOLeNT aCT of RaNDoMNeSS!

***Just Letting Off Some Crazy Steam*** -- *March 2, 2013*
It has been said that just because you **can** watch 16 episodes of *Parks & Recreation* back to back, doesn't mean you **should**. Well, I'm here to say I think that's caca. To maintain my sanity (which is hard), I find it necessary to take a day off once in a while. Yesterday was one of those days. Though some may say my day off had to do more with my *P&R* obsession than my need for a sanity break, all I can say is the first step in dealing with a problem is recognizing that you have one. I'm not ready to do that yet.

Plus I did do a couple other things on my day off, like carving out time to perfect my whistling lips beat box skills. If you think I'm joking, ask my family. They will nod in acknowledgement before bowing their heads in shame.

*(Side note: The picture above is being posted in protest of the "look how cute I am" photomania currently on Facebook. I call this "look at how moronic I am." No extra charge for the fly away hair and dark circles under the eyes.)*

I also coaxed my Action Figure Jesus into turning water into wine. I have to say, he outdid himself. Instead of a standard table wine, he produced a savory full-bodied cabernet with soft vanilla undertones. Yum.

Then to continue the magic, I let my dragon finger puppet friend, Steve, help me type this post. (My index finger had a boo boo and typing hurt. Boy. Such a good friend, that Steve.)

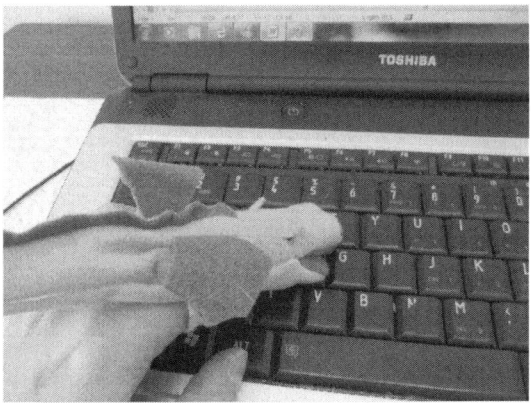

*Steve was rescued from the $1 bin at IKEA. The thought of him languishing in a landfill made me cry.*

And now I feel much better. Sure, I'm still a little crazy but you knew that already.

# CHAPTER 9
## Insecurity Blanket

I hated high school.

There. I said it. It was the worst four years of my life. I don't know about you, but life in that claustrophobic social bubble really sucked for me.

Okay, so maybe it wasn't as bad as I remember. Lucky for me, I found an old chart I'd made. Back in high school I kept a tally of those weeks when I felt particularly blue:

DEPRESSION CHART

|          | SEPT | OCT | NOV | DEC | JAN | FEB | MAR | APR | MAY | JUN |
|----------|------|-----|-----|-----|-----|-----|-----|-----|-----|-----|
| FRESHMAN |      | ▓   |     | ▓▓  |     |     |     | ▓   |     |     |
| SOPHOMORE|      |     | ▓   |     |     | ▓▓  |     |     |     |     |
| JUNIOR   |      |     | ▓   |     |     |     |     |     |     |     |
| SENIOR   | ▓    |     |     |     |     |     | ▓   |     |     |     |

They're marked in gray. ;)

One of my problems was that I wasn't popular, something I really wanted to be. There was just one problem: I didn't really like the popular kids in my school. Now keep in mind, I'm not talking about the genuinely popular kids that everyone liked. I'm talking about kids in the "popular" crowd, which is a totally different animal.

Don't misunderstand me. The kids in the popular crowd at my school weren't all that bad. In fact, some were pretty cool. I just didn't happen to have much in common with them. We liked different things, had different thoughts, plus they moved a bit faster than me -- and I don't just mean that in a figurative sense. I sucked at running the mile.

Regardless, none of that stopped me from my dreaming of being popular. There was a fantasy I used to play in my head all the time. It began the same way each and every time -- with a totally fabulous makeover. A huge sum of money would come my way somehow, allowing me to buy the perfect gear -- the right clothes, the shoes, a Sony walkman to play all my cassettes -- popular kid kind of stuff.

After my transformation into awesomeness, I would walk into the school. A wind machine would be propped up in the corner so it could softly blow hair out of my face. All the boys would "ooh" as the girls dropped their jaws in equal parts admiration and envy. I would be instantly cool.

Then the cute, popular guy I'd lusted after would walk up to me and ask me out. We'd go out on a date where we'd bump into other popular kids at school. I would wow them with my charm, make them laugh with my wit. I'd be accepted into their crowd. From there, I'd discover that the popular kids secretly thought that what *I* liked was cool. Yippee!

There was just one problem with the fantasy. It wasn't real life. Once I opened my eyes I was back to reality. Reality sucked. Of course, we're talking high school reality, which is so unlike real life. After graduation, my whole world expanded. The bubble popped and life was great.

But let's get back to my teenage despair. That's what this chapter is all about. I'll start at the point when I realized something tragic: that I was a dork.

**FEELING LIKE A PHONY**

It was a summer day before the start of my eighth grade year. My friend, and I had met a couple of cute guys at a roller rink. Okay, they might have been losers but they were also two years older than us, making them cool by default. And since my friend had been the prettiest, the cuter of the two guys had given her his phone number. A few days later, while we were hanging out in her bedroom, we decided my friend should call him.

I watched her walk over to her stereo instead of heading to her phone. I asked my friend what she was doing. "Finding some music," she replied.

"Music?" Was she going to dance while she called?

"I need to find the right song to play in the background for the call," she mused while scanning her 8-track tapes.

"Why?" I asked, amateur that I was. "Won't playing music make it hard for him to hear you?"

"I won't play it loud," she said, looking at me like I was a moron. "Just enough for ambiance."

*Ambiance.* I'd look that word up in the dictionary when I got home. As for right then, I'd just roll with things and learn.

A minute later, my friend found the perfect song. Was it Pink Floyd? Led Zepplin? I can't remember. Regardless, she put it on then called the guy during the sweet spot of the song. What a pro, I remember thinking. She knew just what to say to him. All I could do was giggle with nervous excitement, awed by her skill with boys.

Stupid story, huh? I know. I felt lame writing it but what can I say? That phone call was important -- at least it was to me at the time.

But let's fast forward a couple years. It was 1981. I was a high school sophomore. At the time, I had a few friends but no real group to call my own. Then the oddest thing happened. A nice," popular" girl asked me to call her after school. I can't remember the reason -- something about homework, I think -- but I knew she was reaching out to me. I thought that was nice. The fact that she was part of the popular crowd I so ~~loathed~~ longed to be part of added to her appeal.

She had told me to call around four o'clock. Trying to look smooth, I called at 4:01. And then I heard it. The music. Playing softly in the background, it was the perfect song.

Now I'm sure it was a coincidence. Cool kids always listen to cool music, right? And that made me anxious. What if *she* had called *me* while a Preparation-H ad was blaring from my radio? If I was accepted into the cool crowd, did that mean I had to listen to "cool" music all the time? What if a hemorrhoid ad *did* blast from my stereo? Would I become a laughing stock at school?

Dang, that not only seemed like work, it required a skill I just didn't have or want. Keeping up with the popular crowd just wasn't my style. The phone call was one thing -- pretty silly, really -- but I knew it would be the least of my potential problems. All the social one-upmanship that came with trying to climb the social ladder? I had no interest in it at all. I just wanted to be me, not some person trying to make all the right moves just to impress other people.

So I decided to bail on the whole quest for increasing my social status. It seems funny now. I had such a desperate desire to be part of a certain crowd, even though I knew that wasn't the crowd for me.

You know what's funnier, though? The fact that there was even a popular crowd to begin with. You don't really see that anywhere else beyond high school doors. Sure there are groups of people that are friends, but no one keeps score on which groups are cooler than others -- at least not that I can see. If those people exist, I don't know them. They're not part of my life. That's what's so awesome about the world. It's big enough for me to avoid the jerks, something that's harder in high school. I won't lie. Some people are considered cooler than others. That hasn't really changed. What has is the definition of "cool." It's based more on individual people's perceptions and less on general consensus.

### BETWEEN A ROCK AND A SCARRED PLACE

But let's get back to my high school misery. Remember when I mentioned social one-upmanship? You should. It was only a paragraph ago. If not, I recommend ginko biloba. It's supposed to boost your memory. Anyway, to go with the whole popularity theme, I wrote a silly little newspaper article on my blog. It was about a fake major discovery in someone's backyard that really "rocked" the local high school. Take a look:

## Madre Herald
### High School Population Reeling After Popularite Discovery

AP, Atlanta – This past weekend, Shady Maple School District struck gold upon the recent discovery of something many considered a finite natural resource: popularite. Known to increase social status and enhance good looks, popularite was considered so valuable and hard-to-find, many teens went to great lengths to get it. Now that's no longer necessary

"I was digging a hole in the backyard and just stumbled on it," said Charlie Chinklbotz of his find - a chunk of popularite the size of a mini-van. "There's enough for every student in town. Heck, enough for every student in the county! Some people told me I should sell it. I don't need any now that I'm grown. But like most folks, I had some hard times in school, so I'm giving it away for free."

Yes, that's right - FOR FREE.

News of Mr. Chinklebotz's generosity spread quickly, followed by cheers from local high school students. "No one needs to back stab or spread rumors anymore!" exclaimed junior, Missy Henderson. "I'm just glad I can relax and be myself now," said fellow-classmate, Ryan Brown.
But not everyone was thrilled.

"I worked so hard to get my popularite," confessed one teen girl who asked to remain anonymous. "It's not fair that kids can get it now for free." She went on to describe one of many tireless battles she waged to obtain popularite. "Just last year, a new girl entered school right in the middle of the semester. I just knew she'd take some of my popularite without even having to do anything. I had to act fast."

After a carefully crafted smear campaign, highlighted by a nasty rumor stating that the girl slept with a Jimmy Kimmel photo under her pillow, she managed to not only cause undying embarrassment for the new girl, but obtain 1.5 ounces of popularite in the process.

"I always did what it took to keep my popularite – from giving girls the stink eye to flat out bullying and blackmail. No one could stand in my way."

Now, it seems, no one cares anymore and that just makes her mad. "Now that no one's afraid of me anymore, I don't have friends. It's not fair."

How sad.

Now that there's enough popularite for everyone, this reporter wonders what will happen to the now unstable social structure of the student population. Will students begin treating each other better than before? Will teen angst become a thing of the past? I, for one, hope so.

*Popularite in pure form.*
*Many say it looks like "a plain old rock."*

You know, popularity doesn't have to be a limited substance that only a few can have. That's also true for other things like beauty, talent, and brains. There's enough for everyone. That's why the "pulling yourself up by bringing others down" thing is stupid and unnecessary.

Yet there are people who do that and, for some reason, many are girls from 13-17 years of age. Full of backstabbiness and snark, they find great joy in trying to make other girls miserable. Can you only find these girls in the popular crowd? Heck no. The B*itch Fairy blesses girls high and low! *(Side note: I realize I didn't fool you with asterisk. We all know how the "B" word is spelled. So, in essence, I have reneged on my earlier promise not to go blue in this book. And I'm sorry. Truly. It's just I had so much trouble finding another word that captured the essence of my message. If by using it, I've broken our circle of trust, all I can do is beg forgiveness. Let's try to move on.)*

**BULLY FOR YOU!**

A few years ago, MTV had a really cool TV documentary-style show called, *If You Really Knew Me*. Each week they focused on a different U.S. high school, following a group of teens as they participate in "Challenge Day." The day was a sort of huge group therapy session for the entire school. Cliques are tackled and barriers broken, leaving everyone in the end feeling they not only know each other better, but understand each other better, too. I've got to say, it was pretty powerful stuff.

In the spirit of the program, I decided I'm going to share a few special things about my personal life with you. I know. Pretty exciting, huh? I can actually feel the tingle in the air. Here I go:

**1. I hate long talks on the phone**. If we've been talking awhile and I become abrupt, it's not because I don't like you anymore. I'm just ready to pop my eardrums with a spork. On the other hand, I'll talk your ear off in person. I've done it before, ask Van Gogh.

**2. I firmly believe that U2 is, and forever will be, the greatest rock band of all time.** They were a beacon of hope in the otherwise synthetic Eighties and continue to pump out great tunes. Dispute this and feel my wrath!

**3. I was bullied in high school**.

Now as badly as I'd like to discuss the incredible band that is U2,

I'm going to talk about something else. That's right. Let's get right on the telephone issue....

Kidding! I'm going to talk about the bullying. What a surprise. I won't go into details. All I'll say is it was minor compared to some of the things we've heard over the years. There was no made-for-TV movie or special episode on Oprah dealing with my experience. Regardless, it affected me. You know what?

It still does.

I'm no expert on the matter, but from what I've surmised there are three major issues kids have to deal with when they're bullied: fear, lowered self-esteem, and anger.

**The fear**. Luckily, mine wasn't bad. I wondered what would be said or done next, but I didn't fear for my life or worry about physical harm. I wish that were the case for everyone. It isn't.

**The lowered self esteem**. That didn't really happen to me, but I know it happens a lot. In my case, I hardly knew the perpetrators so it didn't take much to realize it was more about them than about me. Having great parents was a big factor, too. They were terrific esteem builders who made home a soft place to land. That's big during the teen years. Bullying can crush a spirit.

**The emotions**. For me it was sadness mixed with a lot of anger. I'm into my forties and still have times where I think about it, relive it. I can't really say I'm still mad at them. I've chosen to forgive. But I did that more for me than them. Hate devours the soul. At the same time, it's something I can't forget. It may sound cliché, but it's true. There are times when it all comes welling back – the feelings, everything. I wish I could say I'm totally over the ordeal. I hope someday I can.

But back to the TV show. Some of the kids who were bullied had really incredible stories. Others have ones that are incredibly ordinary: a struggle with weight, parents getting divorced, simple pressure to just fit in. Regardless of their issue's magnitude or prevalence, everybody hurt.

To compound it all, some kids don't have moms as cool as me. And trust me, that's not very cool. Right now I'm in a white, terry-cloth robe wearing slippers that look like bear claws. How stylish.

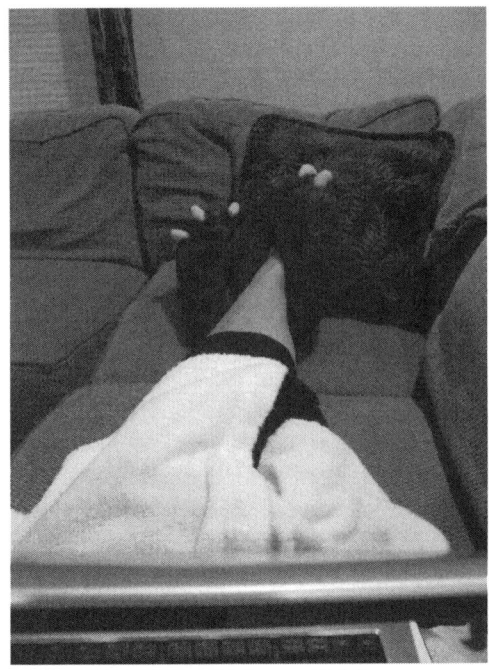

*You thought I was kidding.*

I'd love it if everyone had normal (albeit weird) moms. Unfortunately, that is not the case. Some moms, well… some moms just suck. Not "I don't care if Channing Tatum is signing autographs at the KwikMart, grounded means grounded" kind of suck, but REALLY suck. They can't take care of themselves, much less take care of their kids. Imagine facing a bully with that albatross around your neck. I bet it's not much fun...

But I digress. Back to bullying. I'm curious, if you're still a student, who do you see when you're walking down the school hallway? Someone struggling in the world who could use a little boost? Or do you see a target, someone you can put down to make yourself feel a little better? Or maybe you're not the bully, just a snickering bystander or someone too scared about ruining their reputation to speak up?

Don't think the words spoken – be they loud jeers or quiet whispers – will evaporate as soon as they're said. Words can hang in the air a long, long time. Some never disappear.

You don't care, you might say? That person deserves it? I urge you to think twice. In all my years, I've heard many people say, "I wish I hadn't said that. I wish I'd realized how juvenile I was."

I've never heard anyone regret giving a compliment.

So tell me, how do you want to be viewed? How do you want to be remembered? Because people WILL remember, I guarantee that.

I know because I still do.

### WHAT GOES AROUND...

By the way, did you notice I haven't gone into detail as to what exactly happened to me? It's because I don't want to. Sorry but I'm not in the mood to relive it again. I will say that it involved some sort of nasty rumor about me, as well as inane crank phone calls. One of the things that really make me shake my head was that, fueled by stupidity, one of the girls in the group actually thought I couldn't recognize her voice over the phone. I could. I knew exactly who she was and, by association, knew the others. I'll be honest. I never did learn the rumor they had spread. I just knew that it existed. When my best friend found out the details, she just said, "You don't want to know." And she was right. I didn't really want to know or care. Perhaps I should have cared more. Or maybe cared less? Though I kept telling myself how silly the whole thing was, like I said, it affected me.

It also affected one of the girls, though I doubt she knows that to this day. You see, she ended up going to the same college as me and, during junior year, she applied for a job. Funnily enough, the person who would be her boss just so happened to be one of my best friends. After her interview, my friend called me up and said, "Hey, there's a girl who applied for this job. I noticed she went to the same high school as you. Can you tell me anything about her?" I could, and I did. There was no venom in my voice when I told her what had happened. There didn't have to be. The facts spoke for themselves. Needless to say, the girl didn't get the job.

Many years later, I saw another one of the girls at our twenty-year high school reunion. Imagine my surprise when she came over, gave me a hug and said, "I'm so glad to see you." You know what I did? I hugged her back which, frankly, surprised me even more. I can't say I was thrilled to see her, but the desire to stab her in the eye with a fork had certainly waned. It had been twenty years. I had grown. *She* had grown. We weren't the same people we'd been long ago. That's when I realized I'd truly forgiven her. I mean, I'd done stupid things in high school and had forgiven myself. It only made sense to do the same for her.

Now had my situation been really brutal, things might have gone differently for me. When it comes to bullying cases, I got off easy. Some of the cases I hear these days really break my heart. For those kids who get bullied, all I can say is it's not about you. It's all about them. They are the ones who are broken. They are the ones who need to be fixed. You, on the other hand, are awesome. :)

I've got to say, having that attitude really did help me when I dealt with all of that. At no time did I ever think there was ever anything wrong with me. Okay, that's a lie. Though I was more than comfortable with the person I was on the inside, when it came to the outside it was a totally different story.

## THE EYE OF THE BEHOLDER

Before I get into what I'm about to say, it's important that you know something about me. **I was beautiful in high school.** Did that title get your attention? I thought it might.

The truth is I wasn't bad looking. The only problem was I didn't realize it at the time. Back then, it seemed like there was always something about me that needed fixing. My face, my hair, my body -- I had problems in every department. And I knew if I could change them, I would be perfect and my life would be totally different -- I'd be more popular. I'd get the attention of that cute guy in study hall. I'd meet the girl who played Blair on the TV show *Facts of Life* and she'd let me raid her closet. Yay!

My features are dark, so back in the day I idolized similarly featured teen super model Phoebe Cates. She graced the pages of *Seventeen* magazine on a frequent basis -- that is, until her role in the movie *Fast Times at Ridgemont High* where she played a VERY sexually active teen who took her bikini top off in a rather hilarious dream sequence. She didn't appear in the magazine after that. Go figure.

Anyway, before that movie she was my inspiration. I can still visualize my favorite photo of her. She wore these purple wide-whale corduroy pants with a cinched draw-string waist that were totally rad. Such the style icon. With her image squarely in my mind, I would sit cross-legged on the bathroom counter and analyze my face. I'd think if my eyes were a little bigger, my forehead a little higher, my nose a little smaller, and my chin a little softer I would look *just like her.* And life would be perfect.

Well, a little while ago I chanced upon one of my old high school yearbooks. Biting my nails, I flipped to my picture. Yep, it was me, Eighties hair and all, and you know what? I didn't look that bad. In fact, I looked pretty good. What had I been so uptight about? Skimming through the photos I noticed almost *everyone* looked good. To think of how many lunchroom conversations we wasted talking about what we'd change about ourselves. Stupid.

I wish I would have spent far less time worried about perfection and a lot more time enjoying who I was. Life would have been so much more fun. Even now I have to catch myself. I'm not getting any younger, you know. But I bet when I'm sixty years-old looking at photos of me today, I'll be thinking I didn't look half bad. So do yourself a favor: Next time you look in the mirror, focus on what's right instead of what's wrong. As they say, beauty is in the eye of the beholder. And who do you think is the most important beholder?

That's right, baby. You.

When my kids were infants, I asked myself what kind of people I wanted them to be. One of the most important things I wanted for them was to just be comfortable with who they were. Accepting who you are -- *loving* who you are -- gives you a special kind of armor. It gives you courage to shine, the strength to show the world what you can do.

It enables you to fly.

# ViOLeNT aCT of RaNDoMNeSS!
## A CAT'S TAIL OF DIABOLICAL REVENGE

I can't remember what my sister did. All I know is that it really pissed off our cat, Tiki, and when it came to cats, Tiki was the kind you just didn't want to anger. Ever. Sure, she was sweet most of the time. When she sat on my face while I was sleeping, she did it with love-- not the desire to smother me. When she bit my face because I gave a stray cat some milk, she...oh, who am I kidding? That was flat out rage.

One time my brother, Jim, who was five years-old at the time, picked up Tiki by the tail and swung her around in a circle. In a feat I still consider right up there with Superman, she curled up her tail mid-swing and, you guessed it, bit him in the face. Seriously, though, she was a wonderful cat most of the time. You just had to watch out. If you made her mad and she *didn't* bite your face, you had no idea what might be coming. Case in point: what she did to my sister, Heather. Talk about freaky.

Heather, who was about ten years-old at the time, loved many things. Holly Hobby, Nancy Drew mysteries, and Tang instant breakfast drink are a few that come to mind. Heather also loved her stuffed animals. Right by her bed, she had a cute 18" high wooden bunk bed set where all of them slept. Her favorite teddy bear got the top bunk because, as you know, the top bunk is the coolest. That bear also got a very special bedspread -- Heather's very favorite baby blanket from her infant years. So soft to the touch, the cotton blanket had tiny teddy bears printed all over it. Heather loved that thing and everyone knew it. That included Tiki.

As I said before, I can't remember what my sister did. All I know is Tiki didn't like it. So when we came home one afternoon and found the crime scene, we shouldn't have been so surprised. Yet we were. I still remember Heather's shriek after she'd gone upstairs to her room. I leapt up the steps. Running straight into her room, I stopped short. Then I laughed. Really laughed.

There, on the carpet in the middle of the room, lay Heather's teddy bear blanket. It had been spread out perfectly. Not one wrinkle could be found, but something else could. There, smack dab in the center of the blanket was a pile of Tiki's poop. It must have taken Tiki hours to knead that blanket out. The poop? Probably not so long.

Who knew? Tiki the Cat: criminal mastermind. We never looked at her the same way again.

## CHAPTER 9
## Make Good Choices!

It kills me when I see one of my kids dress all screwy or act in an ill-mannered way. Why? Not just because I'm disappointed in them but because it makes me look like a moron. In my website's section *Why Does Mom Do That?* I explain at length why moms obsess over the way their kids look and act. If you want a simple explanation, though, I can tell you in six easy words: because the mother is always blamed.

"Who raised that kid?" "Who let them out of the house like that?" "Who taught them how to behave?" Whatever question it is, it's always followed by another: "What kind of mother do they have?"

In my case it's not fair because in life you're supposed to reap what you sow, and while my kids have embarrassed me numerous times I have *never* embarrassed my mother. Like that time in high school when we went shopping together, I knew she loved the hairstyle I was wearing. Mirrored after Chrissy from the TV show *Three's Company*, it was quite a glamorous look. Due to licensing, I can't put a photo of her in this book but I can re-create it. Once you see it I'm sure you'll agree it's totally stylin'.

Cool, right? To be fair, the style had only one rubber band -- the one nearest to my head. I had to wedge a nail file in the tail and wrap a second band around it to achieve proper height since my hair is longer now.

Anyway, when Mom and I cruised around together, her cheeks were red with pride, not shame. Sure, she might have said something before we went out, like, "Maybe that hairstyle should be worn only at home." But I didn't listen. Why? Because I was cool and my mom was not.

Seriously, though, the way you look and act can play heavily on your success. The whole "it's what's inside of you that counts" is only half of the truth. For people to see what you've got on the inside, they've got to make sure the outside doesn't scare them away. This chapter will deal with just that, giving you my thoughts and tips on how to look and act so you can be all you can be.

Please note, these tips are primarily aimed at girls. If you're a guy, I'm sorry. Frankly, though, you should have guessed this book was aimed more toward females when I mentioned a maxi pad in the first chapter. If you're a mom (or dad) just sit back and nod or shake your head depending on whether or not you agree.

### MAKING THE (HAIR)CUT

Let's start our focus on look by revisiting that super neato *Three's Company* hairstyle I wore while shopping with my mom. I thought it had been cool because a popular character on a TV show had worn it. There's only one thing I'd forgotten to consider -- that fact that the TV character was a dingbat. Sure, she was a *gorgeous* dingbat, but a dingbat nonetheless. Which is why she wore that hairstyle. What did I say by copying her hair? I was a dingbat, too.

When it comes to appearances, dealing with hair can be one of the biggest challenges. The way it's cut and styled can mean the difference between looking like a goddess and looking like a dork. Luckily, the Marcia Brady long-locks-parted-down-the-middle is fairly popular these days. It's pretty easy to achieve. Back in the Eighties it wasn't so easy. We had to deal with hair spray, curling irons and permanents.

Every woman has a hair horror story stuffed in their back pocket. It's a bona fide fact. Thank goodness we had my dad in our family. He always did a great job of making bad hair days feel not so bad. Like the time my mom came home with a new do that, truth be told, was a little goofy. It put her in a funk until Dad worked his magic right at the dinner table. Studying her hair for a moment, he said, "It's not that bad, really. In fact, it's kind of cool the way it conforms to the shape of your head." His reaction to my sister's hair debacle about ten years ago? "You're hair's so neat. You look just like Jimmy Neutron." Of course my sister, having the driest of humor, responded flatly. "Thanks, Dad. That was the look I was going for."

When it comes to hair success, all I can offer is three snippets of advice: make sure your hair is washed, the style is current, and it looks nothing like Chrissy's from *Three's Company (*or from *Jimmy Neutron*, for that matter.)

### HO!HO!HO!

Let's move on to apparel. As discussed earlier, whether you like it or not, the clothes you wear plays a role in how you are perceived. During my teen years, I experimented with a bunch of different looks in an effort to find out what looked like "me." Most of them were closely tied to the fashion of the day. Not all of them worked. There was the preppie phase, of course, which consisted of doubled up polo shirts -- collars up, of course -- with a sweater draped over the shoulders, its arms tied around my neck. Then I became *Flashdance* girl, as described in an early chapter. I didn't quite pull that one off because my folks wouldn't let me cut out the necks of my over-sized sweatshirt. They thought the shirt-falling-off-the-shoulder thing looked "risqué." I also went through the pre-grunge lumber jack phase -- jeans, flannel shirts, and clunky hiking boots.

It really wasn't until my senior year of high school that I really concerned myself with wearing clothes to attract the opposite sex -- not that I didn't want to look good for guys, it's just that girls cared more (and said more) about what other girls wore. I think there comes a time in most girls' lives when they become more interested in what the guys think. That's when it gets to be a real challenge -- and not just for the girl, mind you. Imagine being the parent.

Like when it comes to dressing like a ho. Oh, come on. You know what I'm talking about. Too much here, not enough there, fishnets paired with thigh high boots -- that sort of thing. Instead of going into the nitty gritty of what's okay to wear and what's not, I'm going to focus on mom's reaction. (Still, for the record, I will say a red bedazzled bra with matching leather mini-skirt is a "don't." The same is probably true for see-through t-shirt dresses paired with fishnet stockings but it really depends on the occasion, right?)

Let's set the scene shall we? Picture a teenaged girl in her bedroom getting ready for a big night out. She looks herself over in the mirror and thinks, "This outfit definitely won't pass the mom inspection. But, still -- dang! I look totally hot! And I am growing up aren't I? Maybe, if I just sneak out the front door…" Deciding to go for it, she sneaks downstairs toward the front door.

That's when she gets busted.

Just as she places her hand on the door knob, her mom strolls into the hall. Her mom doesn't say anything *yet*. The woman just gives her a look that says she's not going anywhere -- at least not like that. Not without a fight. The girl takes a deep breath and prepares for the worst. Here's where I come in. Want to know what the mom is thinking?

For some moms I'll be wrong, but for most I'll be right. Typically, there are two responses:

**Response #1:** *Oh my, GOD! I'm raising a (OMITTED DUE TO ADULT CONTENT FILTERS)! What have I done? What has SHE done? I hope I'm not too late. She needs an intervention! Call the priest/minister/rabbi/appropriate religious figure ASAP!*

You saw that one coming, didn't you? Well, with everything parents hear today are you really that surprised? We're constantly worried about our kids "making the right choices." We know it's a battle. We've been there. Still, you'll find the parents who respond like that are the teeny tiny minority. This next response, though? It's the one most parents think and you just might be surprised. It goes a little something like this:

**Response #2**: *Oh, man. She's reached that age where she's starting to explore her sexuality. Does she realize the way she looks? I hate to say it, but it looks like she's asking for it. That can mean only one of two things…*

She IS asking for it. Please say that's not the case. She's so young, too young. Does she really know what "it" means? I'm not talking about the physical mechanics, but the aftermath-- the consequences, feelings, potential problems? (dramatic pause for reflection) Looks like it's time for a serious talk.

And that outfit? Talk about attracting the wrong attention. She doesn't look alluring, she looks easy. Every boy who sees her will think that way, too. That also goes for the girls.... Oh, man. The girls. I can't wait for the rumors to start. (Sigh.)

Okay, let's not jump to conclusions here. Chances are she's NOT asking for it. She might not realize the kind of message she's sending. I really hope that's it...

Kids must always remember their moms are on their side -- at least most moms are. They want their kids to look their best, feel their best, *be* their best. So what happens next? I don't know. It's up to the girl and their mother. All I can offer is the fantasy that plays in my little mom head:

*The mom gently guides the girl back to her room and helps her pick out an outfit. The two of them find something both attractive and appropriate. They talk about different ways to attract guys without looking desperate. This leads to a nice, heartfelt talk about (ahem) other things and it doesn't feel awkward at all! As they ask and answer each other's questions, they both feel the mother-daughter bond strengthen. The mom gives her daughter a hug and tells her how much she loves her, how she hopes her daughter can come to her with any problem. "Mom," the girl says. "You're so wise. What would I do without you?" It ends with the mom walking the girl to the door. The girl looks beautiful, confident.*

*Now certain her daughter's priorities are straight, the mom smiles, marveling at what a wonderful young woman her daughter has become. The girl gives her mom a sweet kiss on the cheek, opens the door, and dashes to her car. It's a cute car -- not too flashy with a high safety rating that the girl purchased with her own money. As the mom watches her drive away, she wipes a happy tear from her eye. Then she saunters into the kitchen to grab a slice of zero-calorie French silk pie, only to discover the entire room is spotlessly clean, the work of magical fairies.*

Hey, I can dream, can't I?

Anyway, chances are it won't go anything like that. But, as a mom, I really want it to be. Actually, what I REALLY want is to never see girls dressing like a ho. Talk about a dream come true.

## SURE TO HIT *THE NEW YORK TIMES* BEST-SELLER LIST

So remember, what you wear says a lot about you or, rather, what people might *think* about you. It can also give your dad a heart attack and I, for one, don't want that. But skanky outfits aside, what's fun about clothes is how easily they can be changed. You can go from sporty to glam just like that. All it takes is a cute dress and a pound of body glitter.

Some things, though, can't be changed so easily. That's where moms like me get a little worried. Take tattoos. They're really hot right now, but in ten years? I don't know. I've got to admit, I'm not a big fan. Let me explain why...

Frankly, I never gave the subject much thought until Mattel came out with Tokidoki Barbie. Unlike the standard Barbies, this one was pink-haired and had tattoos. I was totally outraged. You heard me. Outraged! The whole thing was just terrible! I mean, come on. Since the 1950's we've counted on the Barbie franchise to not only uphold but glorify the 4 standard B's of beauty: **BLOND** and **BLUE EYES** with **BIG BOOBS**.

After what they did, I feared girls would think there is more than one kind of way to be beautiful. Wrong. And as for the tattoos, themselves? Well, we all know what getting one of those can lead to.

Wait, you don't? Well, then let me enlighten you. Below is a story I wrote. I slapped it together while my youngest was eating his what-kind-of-a-mother-are-you crap cereal before he went to school. For full effect, read along with an *If You Give a Mouse a Cookie* voice in your head. I must warn you, though, it is very disturbing. With that said, here it comes...

*(This section left blank so you're hit with that incredible "wow" factor as soon as you turn the page.)*

# IF YOU GIVE A TEEN A TATTOO
## by Janene Murphy

If you give a teen a tattoo...

She'll start to hang with the wrong crowd.
She'll start skipping social studies class and playing music way too loud.

## MOMS are from MARS

165

Soon she will start drinking, then she'll move to hard core drugs.
She'll not only hang with losers but consort with evil thugs!

*Ugh...I gotsta get me some more crack!*

*Well, then do I have an opportunity for you!*

- disintegrated language
- crack face
- lighter
- empty spoon
- thick gold chain

They'll tell her that they know a way to get her drugs for free.
They'll dress her like a skanky ho and let men play with her for a fee.

"LUV 4 SALE"

- too short faux leather skirt
- low cut, belly exposing see-through shirt
- thigh-high boots that would look cute with skinny jeans, but look slutty with mini skirt

So don't give your teen a tattoo. Perhaps a Barbie Doll instead? She might not be too happy, but at least she won't end up dead!

*Waah! Maybe, if I had given her Malibu Barbie instead of Tattoo Barbie when she was a little girl, this wouldn't have happened!*

THE END

So now you've been warned:
TATTOOS LEAD TO PROSTITUTION AND DEATH.

For those of you who think I am serious, I am about to shock you: I am not. Still, if you do decide you want a tattoo, remember they are permanent. In the Eighties, I thought fingerless lace gloves would never go out of style. I was wrong. A Tweetie Bird tattoo on your ankle might look pretty fun now but when you're 85 years old? Maybe not.

One other thing to consider is that tattoos age, just like you. They don't just get faded, they also change along with your body. That might not be a good thing. A friend of mine once told me about a girl she knew who went to THE Ohio State University. She decided to get a tattoo -- the word "OHIO" in red on her lower abdomen. Years later, she got pregnant and her belly expanded. After she had her kid, her belly went back down. Only her skin had kinda sorta stretched out from the experience. From then on her tattoo no longer said "OHIO." Instead, it looked more like "oHIO."

*Side note:* If you know my mother, you might not believe what I'm about to tell you. Back in the early Seventies she did something unbelievably scandalous. There was a trend that had started -- one that many had thought would die out very soon. My mom didn't care.

She loved it so much she jumped on the band wagon right away. When she showed my aunts what she had done they couldn't believe it. It was so retro. She looked like a gypsy! They swore they'd never do it, themselves. Years later, though, they finally succumbed.

They joined my mom by piercing their ears.

So, who knows? Maybe this tattoo thing will stay popular a good long while. For those with tats, I sure hope so.

## UP IN SMOKE

Before I end the "how you look" portion of this chapter, there's one last item I'd like to address: smoking. You might think it strange for me to put it here in instead of in the "how you act" section but I want you to hear me out first.

You see, I doubt a lot of people start smoking because they're wild about pumping smoke into their lungs. It kills and they know that, yet they do it anyway. Why? Because of how it looks -- because of how they *want* to look. I'll break it down for you:

Smoking is bad for you. Smoking = lung cancer. Every where you go people tell you not to smoke. They throw out words like "addiction" and "death" in an effort to scare you.

Yadda, yadda, yadda.

You see, there is a hidden truth to smoking, a truth no one else will tell you. That is, no one but me. Are you ready? Here it is:

SMOKING is COOL.

You heard me. It's cool. I mean, like Jerry Seinfeld said, cigarettes are like fire in your hand that you can control. Awesome. And not only is it cool, but cool people smoke. Look at Charlie Sheen and Lindsay Lohan. They smoke. And not only are they cool, they're great role models, too. Don't think so? Well, then I have just two words for you: Barack Obama. That's right. The President of the United States smokes. How cool is that? Sure, he never lets himself get photographed doing it. He also says he wishes he could quit and that starting to smoke was one of the worst decisions he ever made. I don't believe him. Secretly, he doesn't want to quit because he wants to stay cool.

Now, now. I know there are a few so-called "negative" issues about smoking out there, ones Anti- Smoking Supporters (also known as ASSes) keep harping about. But, trust me. They're really no big deal. To prove it I'm tackling each one head on. I'll start with the biggest:

**Health.** People keep on saying smoking is bad for you, but did you know smokers only lose an average of seven years from their lives? And that's off the back end, when they're ancient. Sure, that number can vary. Some people can get cancer as early as their mid-forties (like I said, ancient) which is probably close to many moms and dads ages, but who needs parents? Once kids hit their teens they have life all figured out. All parents are good for is nagging, telling kids what to do, making dinner, doing your laundry, giving kids a shoulder to cry on when their boyfriend/girlfriend dumps them. Wait, I'm getting off task. Point is, there's only a small chance that a smoker will die early and leave their children without a parent. No big whoop. There are a few other minor concerns - reduced quality of life, heart problems, circulatory issues, other lung difficulties, as well as one or two ill-effects on unborn babies - but, like I said, they're minor so let's just move on to a more important topic.

**Beauty.** Okay, I'll admit it. Smoking does take a small toll on your appearance. No, I'm not talking about your lungs (they do turn black, but no one sees them). It's the whole "yellow teeth and fingernails" business. Hello? Anyone heard of Crest Whitening Strips? Don't forget nail polish. Sure, your skin turns a little yellow, too…and wrinkly…and leathery. But that just makes you look older, and older is cool. To prove my point, I conducted a little experiment and personally gave a cute six year-old girl a pack of smokes every week for ten years. Take a look at the results:

*before...*

## MOMS are from MARS

*and after*

Amazing, isn't it? Just sixteen years-old and she looks, what -- eighteen, nineteen? *Sweet.*

**Money.** The average cost for a pack of cigs is about $5. Not bad. Start out with a measly pack a week and you're only talking $260 a year. Don't buy an iTouch and you're even *just like that*. Sure, once the whole "addiction" thing takes over, it'll cost more. But that's okay. You should be working anyway. Seriously, you should. Already have a job? Then simply adjust your spending habits. Like buying a car, for instance. Instead of getting that Ford Mustang you've had your eye on, just buy a Toyota Corolla. It may not look as appealing but don't worry -- the additional cool points you get from smoking will make up for the loss of car coolness. Now as you get older, there will be other monetary issues. (Try selling that car after you've been smoking in it. Next, try selling your house.) Health care and home insurance costs are greater for smokers, too. But those are lame things you'll only have to worry about as an adult. That means starting to smoke as a teen is that much smarter!

*(Oh! By the way, the "addiction" thing I mentioned earlier? Not a big deal. Sure, reports say only 2.5% of smokers successfully quit each year, but that's because those people are losers without*

*willpower. They aren't you. YOU can kick the habit, trust me. All those chemicals cigarette companies add to addict people just affect wusses.)*

**The Smell.** A lot of people say cigarette smoke smells terrible. You might think so, too. Maybe it's true, but guess what? The smell is cool. As a matter of fact, I think the real reason people don't like to be around smokers isn't because they stink, but because smokers smell so alluring that just one whiff of them makes others want to smoke, too. No lie. Whoa! I just thought of something! If you smoke, you won't have to buy cologne because you already have your own distinctive smell -- burned-out building. That means you'll actually SAVE money. Take that, money argument!

**The Taste.** Okay, here's the last item on my list. Smokers report that food doesn't taste as good as before they started smoking. Seems smoking deadens the taste buds. Well, never fear because the cigarette industry has responded. Introducing flavored cigarettes! (...Wait. Those were banned in a lot of places. What are they now? That's right...) Introducing flavored *cigarillos*! Some of the flavorings include, French vanilla, cherry, and grape. Yes, grape!! You know, when I was younger, I used to soak lumps of charcoal in grape Kool-Aid and suck on them. Delicious! I bet those cigarillos taste similar. They're a little more expensive than regular cigarettes, but that's okay. Instead of a Toyota Corolla, you can buy a used AMC Pacer. I know, not sexy at all, but come on! GRAPE!

So there you have it. I've turned every possible anti-smoking argument into dust. So go ahead, light up. It'll change your life. And that is a promise.

I'll cut the sarcasm now. Know what I really think of smoking? First let me tell you what I thought when I was a kid. I *did* think it was cool... until I took a puff. Holy yuck!

**CHOKE SIGNALS**

When I was little, my grandma smoked. I loved the elegance of the way she held that white stick of flame in her hand. One day at a family party, I saw her sitting and smoking outside amongst a gaggle of aunts and uncles. I went up to her and asked if I could try it. I'd just turned nine, more than mature enough for my first smoke. Grandma said yes. As she handed the cigarette to me, she said, "Why don't you stand in the center of patio so everyone can see how good you look?"

Seriously? That was awesome! Everyone could bear witness to the super cool kid I truly was. With cigarette in hand, I sashayed to the middle of the patio and placed my free hand on my hip. I looked like one of those models in the cigarette ads who had come a long way, baby! Looking oh so casual I took a puff. The smoke filled my lungs.

And it was SO TOTALLY GROSS. I immediately went into a coughing spasm as everybody laughed. Talk about embarrassment. "See why I'm trying to quit?" Grandma asked. I nodded as I threw up a little bit in my mouth.

But I hadn't really learned my lesson about smoking until much later when I was thirteen years old. One of my friends had a mom who smoked -- a mom who'd been conveniently absent one evening while I was visiting.

It wasn't just me there. A few of our friends had been hanging out at her house. We were just goofing around when I saw a pack of cigarettes on the kitchen counter. And I was a teenager -- finally a teenager -- and I wanted my friends to think I was cool. Sneaking a cigarette from the pack, as well as the lighter next to it, I tip-toed out of the house. Still, I wasn't too stealthy. In the back of my mind, I kinda sorta wanted one of my friends to catch me.

One of them did. My friend found me behind the house carefully puffing the cigarette. She playfully went, "Tsk, tsk. Janene, you're such a bad girl." Her words filled me with a secret thrill. Sure, smoking still tasted awful but at least I didn't cough spastically that time. I was on my way to being truly cool.

But then I thought about it: Is that what cool was? Sucking down super gross smoke to try and impress my friends? Sure, I might grow to like it, but would I grow to like me? I realized what I was doing had nothing to do with smoking.

So I put the cigarette out. My experiment with smoking was truly over. I went back into the house and found my friends in the kitchen eating cupcakes we'd made earlier. I looked around at them. They already liked me, smoker or not. What was I so worried about. Then I popped a cupcake in my mouth. It tasted like ash and I threw up a little bit in my mouth.

Now, as an adult, I think the whole business of smoking is just so sad. For the young kids starting out, I think it's sad because they really seem to think that they look cool when, in truth, they just look lost. As for adults who smoke, it's sad because a huge majority would love to quit but they can't. They're addicted.

But I'll step down from my soap box now. It's time to move on from "the how you look" portion of this chapter. It's time to move on to how people act. Spoiler alert:

Many people act like morons.

And that's too bad because what people say and do profoundly affects people's perceptions of them. I've got to say, I'm really glad I didn't grow up in today's day and age. There are so many more landmines thanks to cell phones and social media. All I can say is, "BEWARE!"

### A WOMAN OF FEW WORDS

A while back, a reader contacted me about a problem so pervasive I found it necessary to respond right away. Here's what she wrote:

*"When I am on the computer or laptop, my mother always tries to see what I am doing. It's very annoying, and it makes me think that she cannot trust me, and I cannot trust her to not look at what I am doing."*

My first instinct was to write an explanation for her mother's behavior ASAP in the *Why Does Mom Do That?* section of my website. Okay, that's a lie. My REAL first instinct was to ask, "What in the world is she doing on her computer that she doesn't want her mom to see?" What can I say? I'm a mom, too.

Anyway, after posting my answer I thought back to my days as a teenager. We didn't have the internet – no emailing, Facebook or Twitter. No cell phones or texting, either. If we put any of our thoughts in writing, it was in a diary stuffed under our mattress.

Personally, after about age twelve I chose not to have a diary. Why? Because the written word could be used as evidence – concrete, couldn't be disputed evidence. If I had something uncomplimentary on my mind, I sure as sugar wouldn't write it down. I'd say it. To my friends. Whom I'd sell out if they passed it along to the wrong person.

My, how the world has changed. The social waters have grown darker and deeper, awash in a sea of text. Not good, my dearies, not good at all. Let me explain via silly re-enactment:

# MOMS are from MARS

SCENE 1:
**The date**: 1980
**The time**: 7:55 a.m.
**The place**: Right in front of Laura's gym locker.
*[LISA stomps up to LAURA with fire in her nostrils.]*

LISA: Hey, Laura. Linda told me you said the only reason Luke's dating me is because I've got big boobs. Thanks a lot.
LAURA: What are you talking about? I told her I hoped he wasn't just dating you on your appearance because you're such a great person inside.
LISA: Oh...that's different. Sorry.

SCENE 2:
**Date**: 2013
**Time and place**: same
*[LISA stomps up to LAURA with fire in her nostrils.]*

LISA: I just talked to Linda. She showed me your text saying the only reason Luke's dating me is because I "have boobs the size of beach balls." Thanks a lot.
LAURA: I, er...ummm.

Difficult to dispute hard evidence, huh?
One of my favorite sayings is, **"Life is tough. Life is tougher if you're stupid."** It amazes me how many people are stupid enough to write certain things down. I'm not just talking about teenagers. Many people have been fired from their jobs due to emails they shouldn't have written. Others have been fired for visiting...hmm, shall I say "interesting" websites while they were on the job, too. So think before you type. It's not a hard rule to follow. It'll keep you out of the defendant's chair, too.

## SEEING THE BIG PICTURE
Of course, words aren't the only thing that can sink you. Photos can do just as good a job. A tiny snap in judgment can disappear in an instant but a snap of the camera can let it live on forever. Not only that, with the touch of a finger it can be sent to anyone, anywhere. How delightful. Don't even get me started on videos. All those scandalous outfits and provocative dancing...No, I'm not talking about the Miss USA Pageant in 2010. You know, the one with the

"tasteful" lingerie photo shoots and (surprise, surprise) subsequent pole-dancing debacle. I mean, come on. How many pageant winners have been caught up in sexy photo scandals lately?

Don't answer that.

So why, might you ask, are stories like this becoming more common? Cell phones, with all their photo/video/straight-to-YouTube capabilities, sure haven't helped. Thankfully, they didn't have them when I was your age. Not that *I* did anything wrong, but I recall a few times when friends of mine engaged in stupid behavior that, had they been recorded, may have come back to haunt them as adults. Just sayin'. As for kids today? They might be surprised by the size of your digital footprint. All those videos and photos being taken while they're goofing around with their friends? They don't just disappear as soon as they hit the delete button. They're out there…somewhere… just ready to be plucked from the grid when you least suspect it.

Now I don't mean to scare kids. Scratch that. I do. But I do it with love. I don't want them to be sitting in an office somewhere, gunning for their first real job, only to have some interviewer pull out a picture of them suggestively straddling a mechanical bull in cut-off jeans and a "Grab ME by the Horns" t-shirt. That would be bad.

So be cautious, people. Be very cautious. I'm not saying don't have fun, just don't have *too* much fun when a camera is pointed your way. Which leads me back to the whole scandalous outfits and provocative dancing thing. Ugh.

On April 10, 2010, the World Dance competition took place in Pomona, California. It made quite a news splash when it happened, thanks to one of the dancing acts. It featured seven year-old girls dressed like hoochie mamas dancing suggestively to Beyonce's "Put a Ring On It." That's right. Just seven years-old and their self-worth is already being tied to their sexuality. How sweet. What's next, lingerie photos shoots and pole-dancing? Another question I don't want answered.

Here's what really got me: The girls danced well. In fact, they danced *incredibly* well. Dare I say they rocked? Only I didn't see that. All I saw were a bunch of little girls shaking their boom booms in sexy costumes. Their value as dancers? Suddenly devalued. Devalued like the girl who busted her butt in college to get a 3.5 GPA, only to be told she wasn't qualified to work for Acme, Inc. due to…ahem, unbecoming photos taken during Spring Break '09.

So, once again, be careful out there. Very careful, particularly if you are a girl. Trust me when I say that #1 on the *Top Ten Things That Have Never Been Said* list is: "I'm so glad I made that *Girls Gone Wild* video!" Plus, if I ever see you in one, you're going to get a SERIOUS time out. So do me a favor and always keep in mind Big Brother's out there and he's armed with an iPhone.

### LEAVE NO WILD CHILD BEHIND

I know. It's sad. Today it's hard to let it all hang out without fear of total embarrassment. One lapse in judgment can lead to a whole lot of headache and heartache down the road. I, for one, think that sucks, though when you're out with your buddies it's always good to be on your toes. A night out with friends can turn from fun to terribly tragic in one misstep. But never fear! I found some special guidelines to help you avoid undue tragedy.

Called the **Leave No Wild Child Behind Act**, it was brought in as companion legislation to the Leave No Child Behind Act of 2002. It focuses on behaviorally-challenged females in non-academic situations, mandating the following:

If a female has rendered herself judgment-impaired, be it via a lemonade-induced malaise or simple case of temporary stupidity, under no circumstance should they be abandoned or given the go-ahead to engage in activity that may result in their harm, harassment, or future embarrassment. Examples include but are not limited to:

- Going to a party and accepting a proposal to enter the party giver's parent's bedroom or otherwise private, confined space with a member of the opposite sex whom they do not know well, even if they have been crushing on that person for a while.

- Meeting someone at a party/game/7-Eleven parking lot and deciding they seem okay enough to take a quick ride in their car.

- Meeting someone at a party/game/7-Eleven parking lot and deciding they seem okay enough to accompany during a quick walk around the block.

- Meeting someone at a party/game/7-Eleven parking lot…blah blah blah, you get the idea:

**girl + guy + isolated environment + impaired state = bad.**
**girl + guy + isolated environment + no impaired state?**
**Sorry. It still equals stupid.**

Additionally, under no circumstances should said female be allowed to pose in any state of undress in front of a photo device. This includes video cameras, cell phones, and the security camera embedded in the ATM outside of Walgreens.

Please note, this individual may not be judged by the quality of their appearance, the amount of lemonade they have consumed, or any statements they may have made prior in the evening. In addition, any statements or claims made by the individual during their attempt to proceed, to include, "I know what I'm doing," "Go on without me, I'm fine," or "Leave me alone, you're not my mother," will be rendered insufficient cause to continue.

On the flip side, if the phrase, "She deserves what she gets," is uttered at any time by a female witness in close proximity to the situation, said female is to be dubbed a traitor to their sex and shunned until such time as they make amends.

I know we all act stupid on occasion and sometimes what we fantasize about in our heads ends up being a downright scary situation in reality. That certainly was the case when I was young but I NEVER let my fellow females down. We've got to protect each other. As rock legend/sage advisor, Pat Benetar, once said: love is a battlefield. Girlfriends are your fellow soldiers. When you go out as a team, you return as a team, **leaving no wild child behind.**

And there you have it -- a huge buttload of wisdom on how to look and act wrapped up and tied with a bow. You may not have learned anything but at least I got it all off my chest. Now I'm ready to move on.

## ViOLeNT aCT of RaNDoMNeSS!

**TOO ANGRY TO POST A PHOTO!**

***PMS Alert*** -- *January 26, 2012*
I'm PMSing, so you'd better watch out. I get pretty volatile. And right now I'm **ENRAGED**. It's not my fault, though. Some horrible things have happened to me. Instead of exploding, I'm sharing them with you now. Hold on to your fedoras...

First, I sat down to read the comics this morning and **Sarge beat the living snot out of Beetle Bailey AGAIN.** I'm sorry, but the humor found in the cyclical abuse of a defenseless underling by an authoritarian figure is lost on me. People living in abusive relationships must really yuck it up when they see that, huh? I mean, jeez! If I wanted to get depressed I'd be reading Funky Winkerbean. Throw the handcuffs on Sarge and lock him up in jail already. Sheesh!

Later, on *Who Wants to be a Millionaire,* **Meredith Viera was so much more sadistic than usual.** She did the whole I'm not sure if that's the right answer frowny face thing, only to morph into a giggly grin and say, "That's right!" almost every single time. For God's sake, woman, stop playing with our emotions! My sanity is hinged on the knowledge that Damascus is the capital of Syria. Don't mess with me!

Then there's my microwave. 4 minutes and 23 seconds to reheat four ounces of pasta primavera? Really? Either **the special heating sensor fairies think I have a steel - coated esophagus** or they're out to get me. Strike that. I KNOW they're out to get me.

To top things off, that stupid 1980s Pantene commercial featuring Kelly LeBrock saying, **"Don't hate me because I'm beautiful"** keeps playing in my head. I didn't hate her because she was beautiful. I hated her because she was narcissistic enough to say that in front of a camera. Have some humility, will ya?

By the way, that Eighties hair doesn't look so beautiful now, does it, Ms. LeBrock? I bet eight or nine squirrels could live in those massive curls of wonder.

Whoa. Sorry. That was really snarky. Blame it on the PMS...

Anyway, now I'm sure you understand why I'm a little off today. There's only so much ridiculousness I can handle. Now I'm going to scoop some peanut butter out of the jar with my bare hands and dip it into a bag of chocolate chips.

# CHAPTER 11
# Vacation Frustration

Here's the deal: For a while, I'd been wracking my brain trying to come up with a theme for this last chapter. At the same time, I'd been scrambling to get my family ready for this year's Spring Break vacation during. Suddenly, the light bulb hovering over my head exploded with light -- not a literal explosion. That not only would have killed me but would have left a terrible mess. Not good.

Anyway, I saw the light and realized what I should discuss: the ~~horror~~ wonder that is family vacations. So below please find my notes from our recent trip to New Orleans, Louisiana.

We drove, of course. We're driving people, though we have taken plane trips once or twice. But there's nothing quite like traveling the open road in a car filled with family. Though, keep in mind, the same can be said about swimming in shark-infested waters with rib-eye steaks strapped to your arms and legs.

I'm going to start at the beginning -- the *way* beginning -- by sharing what family travel was like when I was young. You wouldn't think there'd be too many differences between today and yesterday but a few things do come to mind. If you're young, reading these facts will lift you to a higher level of enlightenment (lie). If you're old, like me, it will make you nod nostalgically in remembrance (no lie).

### BACK IN THE DAY: FAMILY TRAVEL

When I was a kid, most of our family travelling was done between the mid-Seventies and mid-Eighties. Back then families rarely flew on a plane. In relative dollars, air fare was about twice as much as it is now. Gas for our cars? Much cheaper. If you went on vacation, chances are you had to drive just as we had.

The car ride? Boy, it was different than today. First of all, we had freedom. Seat belts had been in cars for years, but people didn't use them often. That is, until 1984, when states started passing seat belt laws. There also weren't many car seats. Those came in the mid

Eighties, too. Young kids used something similar to a booster seat. When we were babies, our parents put us in little beds that were held steady by a big prong that nestled into the back seam of the seat.

Scary.

While travelling, kids held reign over the entire area behind the car's front seat. In our family, we got half of the cargo area of our station wagon, so we made a "fort" and took turns using it. There were three of us, so the remaining two had to share the large back seat. It looked like a couch. There were no bucket seats. Up front, the driver/front passenger seat was the same. There weren't two seats with a break in the middle -- no cup holders or storage compartments. In fact, there were no cup holders at all. There were ash trays which -- in our case, at least -- went unused. When cup holders replaced them, we rejoiced.

What did we do in the car? We had no Gameboys or Nintendo DSs. There were no iPods or portable DVD players, either. In fact, few cars had anything more than a radio, maybe an 8-track tape player. Later on cars had cassette players. How luxurious. For fun we would read, write or draw, or look for license plates from other states. We would also play the Alphabet Game, where we'd hunt for letters of the alphabet in order on billboards, road signs and other cars.

Speaking of billboards, they were plastered everywhere. There are much fewer of them today. That's because we didn't have those blue FOOD and LODGING road signs that listed businesses at every exit. A pat on the back goes to whomever came up with that idea. Not that there were tons of food options anyway. Highways had no fast food at every turn. There are twice as many McDonalds now as there were back then. We always had sandwiches in a cooler.

One other thing I remember was all the trash along the road. People chucked their junk out the window. You'd even see garbage bags in the ditches. It was just plain gross. The Crying Indian changed all that. If you don't know about this American icon, look him up on YouTube. He was an institution. With his help, the "Keep American Beautiful" movement took off. No one wanted to be a litter bug.

But let's get back to technology. There were no ATMs, though credit card use had become fairly common. Still, many used cash and Traveler's Checks, both of which you got at your bank.

As for cell phones? I wish! If your car broke down, things looked grim. Instead, there were pay phones at every major business. Hotel reservations were made in advance. That is, unless you wanted to try your luck, which many people did. One year, while my family was travelling home from Colorado we drove home without a plan. On the west side of Kansas, we started looking for a hotel. All of them were booked. It took three hours and quite a few miles before we finally found a motel. The seedy place charged by the hour. My mom instructed us not to touch anything and refused to let us crawl under the sheets. We spread our coats on the bed and slept on top of them.

GPS devices didn't exist, either. Everyone used maps. There was no internet, so there was no MapQuest or a quick way to find hotels. Mobil, AAA and Fodor all had guidebooks with listings of hotels and attractions for every region. Hotel chains also had books of their own. That's the way we got information. One thing we did have that you don't see much now was a "fuzz buster," or radar detector. It detected when cop cars were near by, so drivers could slow down and not get caught speeding. Did I mention they were illegal?

Well, that's the extent of what I remember. Did you notice two odd things about what I wrote? The first thing is that I misspelled the word "traveling," using two l's instead of one. While editing this book, I came to discover that's not how we do it in America. It is, however, how they spell it in Britain and Canada, so I decided to keep it as a nod to my huge international following which is, at last tally, eleven people.

The other thing you may have noticed is back then the trip started, well, when the trip started. The first day of the trip I just hopped out of bed and went straight into the car. But that's only because I was a kid. As a mom, the trip starts long beforehand. There are clothes to pack, snacks to buy, mail and newspapers to stop. It's an excruciating, behind the scenes process that no one fully appreciates until they do it themselves. However, now that I'm a grown up, I can skip the one thing I dreaded doing as a kid. Every year, right after summer, I'd have to write a paper for school entitled, "What I Did During Summer Vacation." Funny thing is, now that I'm an adult, I kind of like writing them, as well as sharing them with you. In fact, I'll share one with you now. Turn the page.

Janene Murphy
August 3, 2011

## My Summer Vacation

I just got back from a ridiculously hot, but fun, family vacation. The theme was American history. We hit Philadelphia, Washington, D.C. and Williamsburg, spending the most time in good 'ole D.C. I've got to say, I learned some new things about our nation's capitol. Here is my report:

**Fun Fact #1: Andrew Jackson loved to party,** and he partied plenty in the White House. Inviting everyone from dignitaries to the local riff raff, our seventh president held numerous public receptions. My favorite? The Great Cheese Party. Featuring a 1400 lb. wheel of cheese in the center of the room, people were encouraged to nibble on it while they socialized.

**Fun Fact #2: John Wilkes Booth wasn't just any actor.** He was THE actor of the day. When he shot Abraham Lincoln at the Ford Theater, it was the present day equivalent of Brad Pitt popping off Obama. I wonder how *Ye Olde National Enquirer* covered that news story...

**Fun Fact #3: Star Wars permeates Washington, D.C.**
**Evidence - The National Cathedral**

One of the gargoyles on the church's façade looks suspiciously like Darth Vader, don't you think? Even more disturbingly, at the time I took this picture, the gargoyle was located on the *dark side* of the church. Coincidence? I think not!

**More Evidence -The National Museum of American History, First Ladies Exhibit.**

It might just be me, but Mamie Eisenhower's hairstyle looks an awful lot like Princess Leia's. Could George Lucas have gotten his inspiration from her? Maybe. (And by the way, museum curators, placing Nancy Reagan's less-than-zero-sized inaugural dress next to Barbara Bush's considerably larger one, though historically appropriate, is cruel. Just cruel.)

**My Final (though I'm SURE there is more out there) evidence - The National Museum of American History AND The Air and Space Museum's gift shops**

Star Wars merchandise everywhere! This includes the kitchy-coolest hoodie currently on the market. Here's my son, gleefully modeling the Darth Vader one:

And, no, he does not share the same stature as an ewok. The only size left was a XXL, meaning all but the largest of men-children have chosen to indulge their latent geeky tendencies.

**Fun Fact #4: The Star Spangled Banner is frickin' HUGE.** Originally 30 feet x 42 feet, the flag that inspired our national anthem is still a whopping 30'x 34' today. Each of its 15 stars is two feet wide. Same with its 15 stripes. Why 15? Because by the War of 1812 two more states had joined the union, Vermont (1791) and Kentucky (1792). The original plan was to add both a star AND a stripe for each new state that joined the union, but they soon realized it had the potential to get way out of hand. The third Flag Act of 1818 changed the number of stripes back to the original 13 to pay homage to the original states.

So there you have it. The educational part of my paper is done. If you are interested in a few trip tidbits of a more personal nature, read on...

**The most disturbing breaking news while away:** The horrible tragedy in Norway. 92 dead due to one troubled man. It not only made me sad but really shook me up.

**The second most disturbing breaking news while away:** The introduction of Breast Milk Baby, a toy doll that comes with a special halter top so children can simulate breast feeding. What's next, a play kit called My First Period?

**Most disturbing thing I saw on the trip:** A woman walking in front of me on the sidewalk who -- oh my god, please tell me she at least had a thong on-- had on these tiny white shorts that were so tight they COMPLETELY went up her butt crack. Got that image firmly planted in your mind? Good. Consider it my gift to you.

**I was witness to an instant loss of credibility:** While my family was casually walking past the White House, history was being made! A protest against deportation was being held, complete with chants and picket signs. It was pretty cool to watch. One sign that stood out to me was neon green, held with pride by a tall young man. I'll be honest, I didn't read the saying on the front. I was too mesmerized by the words on the back. Spray painted in white were the words *Car Wash*. Huh. Now I'm not going to get into the politics of the situation, but will suggest that if you're going to go all big time and demonstrate in front of the White House, head over to your local craft supply store and purchase a new poster board. Seriously.

**The trip keepsake I will treasure for all of my years:** My black coffee mug featuring a mutton-chopped Elvis Presley shaking hands with then president, Richard Nixon, at the White House. I actually went "Squee!" in the National Archives gift shop when I saw it. My kids' faces grew red in horror when they heard me -- double bonus!!

## LOUISIANA OR BUST

Okay, enough with the past. It's time to give you what I promised: an excruciating blow-by-blow of our recent vacation. Sit back in your Barcalounger and relax. It's going to be a bumpy ride.

**Friday, March 15, 2013** - After promising to get on the road by 8 AM, we roll out of the driveway at 9:30. As everyone straps themselves in nice n' tight, we notice the temperature gauge reads 35 degrees Fahrenheit. We can't wait to see it rise as we venture south. Goodbye Iowa! Excited to finally be leaving, we groan when half way down the road when a kid makes an all-too-predictable announcement: They forgot the car charger for one of their electronic devices. We head back toward the house.

Five minutes later, we're back on the road and the car is filled with excited chatter. We're a family! We're on vacation! We love being together! That lasts about five minutes. Then faster than a roadrunner on speed, we each isolate ourselves in technology bubbles. One kid is on a Kindle, another on a Nintendo DS, while the third is on an iPod. Rick starts listening to the 32-hour audio tape equivalent of one of those black and white documentaries you see on the History Channel late at night. I, on the other hand, go old school and read a hard bound book. They still exist, you know.

Later that day, we stop for lunch at Lambert's Cafe in Sikeston, Missouri. It's "the only home of throwed rolls." Of course, that means it's not the home of precise grammarians, but we are quick to forgive. Once we're seated at our table, one of our kids can't wait to catch a roll that's been tossed across the room by a waiter. He signals the waiter. The waiter chucks a roll from forty feet away. He misses. The roll lands on the floor. No worries. They try again and our kid scores. He says the roll is delicious. Later on, he signals for another roll. The waiter obliges and nails him in the middle of the forehead. Thanks goodness, he laughs.

Another waiter comes around and asks if we'd like to try fried okra. To my kids' credit, they politely decline. Still, though their words are kind, they look at her as though she's just offered them dead hamsters on a stick. Feeling bad, I tell the waiter, "I'll have a few!" and then proceed to eat ten deep fried nuggets. As they sink into my stomach, I also get the sinking feeling I will regret my decision. Forty-five minutes later, I do. I will say no more on this issue.

Hours later, we arrive late just outside of Memphis. Did I mention it's 73 degrees outside? Suck that, freezing cold Iowa! This trip is going to be awesome! Plus our hotel room is nice here, too. Still, the floor of the kitchenette area is awful slick. I warn the kids to be careful. This of course, gives free license for one of my kids to disobey my orders entirely. This time it's Paul. Mocking me, he hops over to the floor and starts to dance, going all Michael Jackson with jazz hands. I shake my head. His grin widens until fifty seconds later he lands hard on his butt. Routine over.

**Saturday, March 16** -- We wake up early and continue driving south. Soon we're in good 'ole Mississippi, The Magnolia State. The citrus green outside screams, "It's Spring!" Man, I'm loving the warmer weather. I see a billboard touting its local hospital's award for being "one of the top 40 cleanest hospitals in the United States!" Now that's something to brag about! Pure marketing genius.

We stop at Vicksburg National Military Park to drive around one of the critical battlefields in the Civil War. Very cool. Then we engage in one of our least favorite activities: deciding where to eat. Regardless of where we decide, someone always ends up unhappy. This time it's Mary. Paul snickers when she complains about our choice for lunch: McDonald's. She's not a huge fan of the place. To her luck we end up at a Sonic, instead. which is not one of *Paul's* favorite dining places. When he starts to complain, we mention his laughing at Mary when we thought we'd be eating at McDonald's. From the driver's seat, Rick says, "Sometimes life sucks, Paul. Other times, like now, it's just cleverly ironic." Paul didn't appreciate the humor.

Continuing south, we drive along the Natchez Trace Parkway. The beauty is absolutely astounding. Not astounding enough, however, for the kids to look up from their gaming devices. We tell them to put them away. Bickering ensues, as predicted. Then Rick and I become uber evil. Turning off the road, we force the kids out of the car for a hike along the actual Natchez Trace. It's a grueling trek -- almost one hundred yards! The kids gripe the entire time. As Rick and I do our best to enjoy the surroundings, the kids threaten to call Child Protective Services. It's their vacation, too, don't you know. Why can't they spend it the way they want to? We head back to the car, defeated.

We do end up hitting the jackpot, however, when we make hotel arrangements for the night -- free breakfast and internet for only seventy dollars! What a deal. We grow less enthused when we arrive to discover the place is a motel. We don't have luck with motels.

As soon as Rick gets the keys, a Department of Corrections van pulls into the parking space next to us. We calmly tell our kids we think we'll take the entire contents of our car into the room tonight. They don't ask why.

When we settle into the room, which is surprisingly okay in appearance, I flip open the motel's information manual. Inside, I see a page called "Safety Tips." This is what it says:

*1. Do not invite **STRANGERS** to your room for any reason.*

*2. Close the door securely whenever you are in your room and use all of the locking devices that **HAVE** been provided.*

*3. Don't answer the door in a hotel or motel without verifying who is there. If the person claims to be an employee, call the front desk and ask if someone from their staff is supposed to have **ACCESS** to your room and for what purpose.*

*4. Do not needlessly display guest room keys in public or draw attention **TO** yourself by displaying large amounts of cash or expensive jewelry.*

*6. Do not leave valuables in **YOUR** vehicles.*

*7. If you are traveling with **CHILDREN**, provide adult supervision and know their whereabouts at all times.*

Yikes! A while later, we discover the toilet isn't flushing properly. I lift up the tank's lid. A tube pops up and spews water all over the bathroom. Luckily, it's clear. I find where the tube goes then grab every towel I can find to sop up the water. Still, the toilet doesn't work. We call the front desk and ask for assistance. It takes an hour and a half and three separate visits from the maintenance man before it's fixed. At 11 PM, we're finally able to go to bed.

**Sunday, March 17th** -- We wake up and are so ready to leave. All we want to do is shower, eat, and get out of there. But we need towels. All but one was used to soak up the water from the toilet. Rick tracks down the maid, who politely tells them they have no towels to spare. I shower anyway. As I dry myself off with the one remaining 6" x 6" wash cloth, I think, *Seventy dollars. What a bargain.*

We drive on, finally making it to Louisiana! Before heading into New Orleans, we visit a plantation. Called Oak Alley, it's the famous one where *Cat on a Hot Tin Roof* was filmed. It's also where a craft fair is currently being held. We tour the mansion then go outside and walk through rows of artists' booths. Their stuff looks similar to things we see at other craft fairs across the USA, only with more fleurs-de-lis.

Afterward, we head to the town of Metairie, just outside of New Orleans. Some old friends of ours live there. We meet them at Zea's, a restaurant that has the best grits I've ever eaten, though the only other grits I've ever eaten were Quakers' Quick Grits. Seriously, they are AMAZING, though I'm worried they're 1000 calories per serving. (Later that night, I go online and check. Whew! There are only 864.)

At this point, I must say that throughout the trip so far I kept thinking, "Dang! The kids are being so good. I'm so proud of them. They're really growing up." Well, while sitting at Zea's with our friends I wasn't thinking that at all thanks to my wonderful son, Peter.

Sitting at the table right next to him is our friends' son, who is the same age as Peter. Instead of talking to him, my son whips out his iPod and proceeds to ignore the other boy. Rick and I signal for him to stop. He shakes his head. We persist. He puts down his iPod in a huff. Then he announces for all to hear, "You always assume that because your friends with the parents that I'm going to be friends with their kids. Well, we don't have much in common."

How sweet.

Our friends say they understand but I know they're just being nice. That leaves Rick and me feeling like Parents of the Year. Thank you, son. You're awesome.

That night at the hotel we are beat. After last night's motel disaster we can't wait for a peaceful night's sleep. Which means the kids are awful. Refusing to go to bed, they find bugging each other to be much more fun. But, eventually, they cave into exhaustion, allowing Rick and I to blissfully nod off to sleep.

Until we're woken by an alarm. From its tone we can tell it's signaling an imminent toxic waste catastrophe or a hotel fire. Only it's neither. It's Paul's iPod. As a joke, he'd set his alarm to go off in the middle of the night to scare his siblings. It didn't work, though. None of the kids woke up, including Paul. But Rick and I did. Argh!

**Monday, March 18th** -- Some friends of ours from home are also in town, set to go on a cruise later that day. We meet them at Morning Call, the place New Orleans beignet purists say is better than Cafe du Monde. The beignets come plain so we have to powder them ourselves. I grab the powdered sugar container. Then the counter in front of me turns from brown to white as I coat not just the beignet, but everything else around me. As for my face, I look like a junkie right after a cocaine induced frenzy.

Since it looks like it'll be the best day for weather -- 78 degrees and sunny! -- we decide to book a bayou tour. Exactly twenty three minutes after we give our credit card information over the phone, the sky clouds over. It starts to drizzle. But we've already paid, so we head out to the bayou and reach our destination. Entering the gift shop we see a wide array of lovely souvenirs for purchase.

Luckily, right as our tour starts, the clouds part and the sun shines down on us. We have an awesome time spotting wildlife and feeding alligators and wild boars all the marshmallows they care to eat. We also learn that the fleur-de-lis, the official symbol of Louisiana, is based off a stylized iris lily, which grows wild in the bayou. (As a side note, that is the only educational content in this story. If you're a teacher, I am sorry.)

That day, we finally arrive in New Orleans, just outside of the French Quarter. The kids want to relax in the hotel room. Rick and I don't. We get them a pizza then head out to dinner alone. Worried our kids will find some strange way to get themselves in into trouble, we come home early. Stepping into the hotel room, we find the kids -- gaming devices in hand -- haven't moved from the spots where we left them.

**Tuesday, March 19th** -- Our family sees it all. Getting up early, we hit the National Park Service Tour, then hit the French market where I find some fun voodoo dolls. Though I don't believe in any spooky business -- ghosts and voodoo dolls, included -- I can't resist buying my new friends. Meet Harold and Maude. In the middle is their marriage counselor, Lord Doomsday.

We see Jackson Square, St. Louis Cathedral, then discover the Ursuline Convent is serving lunch because it's St. Joseph's Day. The nuns laid out a feast for the public. As part of said public, we ate it. Yum!

We continue seeing sights. It's such a warm, beautiful day, which is why I'm surprised when I catch a chill. I'm near a fireplace inside the oldest building in New Orleans which now happens to be a pottery museum. I ask if anyone else is cold. They just look at me weirdly. Shrugging them off, I go outside and warm up.

We decide mid-day might be the only safe time for the kids to take a stroll down Bourbon Street. I rethink our decision when I see all of the unusual t-shirts for sale, including one featuring a kinda sorta Hello Kitty motif with the "K" substituted by a "T." As for the advertisements displaying nude women? None of my kids saw those. That's our story and we're sticking to it.

All over the French Quarter, we see evidence of the big party held days ago on March 17th, St. Patrick's Day. Green feathers can still be found in sidewalk cracks, as though a Muppet had been murdered there and the clean up crew missed it. I even spotted some leftover beads in some unlikely places. I think the guy on this statue is asleep because he partied too hard.

That night we go to see the Preservation Hall Band. After waiting in line for over an hour, we're shuffled into a tiny room. It's standing room only and we're stuffed in the back. We cannot see a thing. But we can hear and the music is wonderful. We take advantage of the crowd, which is pressed up toward the front. That means there's plenty of room in the back to dance, so we do. Lemons into lemonade.

**Wednesday, March 20th** -- Rick is giddy beyond belief. Today's the day we go to the World War II museum. It's amazing. We spend many hours there before leaving. Well, four of us leave. Rick stays two more hours. It's history come alive, people!

When Rick gets back, we decide to do one last cool thing during our last night in New Orleans: a haunted tour of the French Quarter. We quickly grab dinner then head over and take the tour. It's a big hit. Our tour guide, Jerry, is a riot. He takes us from place to place, telling us chilling stories of what happened where. One of our last stops is a museum -- *the* museum where I experienced a chill. He proceeds to tell us there's a particular room where many strange things have occurred. People have died. There have been sightings. In fact, if you stand by a certain fireplace you might experience a chill. My jaw drops. He's describing the place where I got suddenly cold, which makes me FREAK OUT BECAUSE GHOSTS ARE REAL-- ***REAL***, I SAY!!!

That night, we have fun walking back to the hotel, stopping in shops and just goofing around. The trip has gone very well, mostly because the kids have been so awesome. I feel so lucky to have them.

**March 21st** -- My kids suck. Okay, maybe it's my fault for keeping the kids out way too late. This morning they not only refuse to get up but when we ask them to help us pack up they whine. It's definitely time to go which, luckily, is what we're planning to do in a few short hours. Our last stop is St. Louis Cemetery No. 1, a cool place where a voodoo queen has been buried. We check it out. By her tomb are offerings people have given her. Sticks of gum and lip balm seem to be the major gifts of choice. Huh.

We head back to that museum where I got that chill. Unfortunately, the spirits aren't playing today. But a person working there gives us a fun mini ghost tour and shows us creepy cool stuff we had missed before. Then we head to Mardi Gras World and see the ginormous parade floats. One of my sons takes an affinity to an old bust of Michael Jackson which, strangely enough, also seemed to develop a skin condition.

And no, my son didn't go all gansta. That bling around his neck serves as the admission ticket. Then we leave New Orleans. Boy, what an adventure! We drive all day until we hit Memphis. It's a balmy 50 degrees Fahrenheit. I want to turn around right then and there and head back to New Orleans. Mama doesn't like the cold.

**March 22nd** -- Before our final drive home we visit Graceland, the place Elvis Presley called home. The place is kitschy kitschy cool. Strangely, they only let us see the bottom floor of the main house because "it was his family's sanctuary. No one was ever allowed upstairs." Yeah, right. I'm sure the real reason is because he's still alive and needs somewhere to live. They're not fooling anyone.

With just a few hours more to go on the journey, I start to feel a little sad. As we've moved north, the world is colder and less colorful. I wish the trip would never end.

Then I see her. Remember in the chapter on fashion where I talk about jeggings? If I recall correctly, I said that the trend hasn't yet produced a tragedy. I was wrong. She stepped out of the gas station wearing a snugly fit white long-sleeved t-shirt. No problem there. But her bottom half wore extremely tight hot pink jeggings. It looked like two sausage links had eaten a topographical map of the Appalachians. I must repeat my plea: SAY NO TO JEGGINGS!

And that's it -- not just the end of my family's vacation but the end of this ridiculous book. Before I go, allow me to leave you with one more post. I know. I just don't know when to shut up.

Seriously, whether you're young or old, this is one I would like you to take to heart. Why? Because in the end, good or bad, it's all about family -- at least it is for me, lucky soul that I am. Sure, there have been tears, but there have also been laughs -- many laughs -- and I thank my family for it. Plus they've been such good sports, not just with my blog but with having me as a mom/wife/daughter/sister/aunt/niece.

Poor things, every last one of them. ;)

## ***Life is Short? Not if You Do it Right*** -- *December 22, 2010*
**"Life is short."**

We hear that all the time. And, yes, there are people out there who, through tragic circumstances, have their lives cut short. But for many of us? Let's be honest. Life is very, very *long*.

Still, the rumors are true. As you get older, time seems to fly by faster. Why is that? I'm not exactly sure. I think as I get older, I "experience" less. Yep, I'm talking about the whole "stop to smell the roses" thing.

I'll be honest. I've stopped to smell the roses many times. I know what they smell like and, frankly, Christmas is coming hard and fast and I've got a boat load of presents to wrap RIGHT NOW. I don't have time. I'm livin' in the fast lane, people!

Here's the thing, though. **While life, in truth, is very long the special moments are not.** They're short. If you don't take the time to stop and savor them, they disappear. They fade away. They become a blur on the highway.

This holiday season I'm giving myself a very special gift: time. I'm going to slow down, engage all my senses and soak in every moment I can.

Now if you're a teen, you might think that's a stupid idea. Savor the holidays? Come on! Your folks are lame and the last time you checked, your baby brother was still a booger. You don't want to slow down time. You want to speed it up. You can't wait to grow up and get out of the house. That's when your *real* life will begin.

Don't fall into that trap. Because once you grow up and leave the house, there will be another goal you'll feel pressured to zoom toward, another stage of life to race through.

Life is not a race. When you hit the finish line, there's no trophy for being first. Remember that this holiday season. Remember that afterwards, too.

With that being said, I'm signing off. My kids are on their winter break and I want to enjoy every minute with them. Why don't you get off the internet and spend quality time with your family, too? Trust me, you won't regret it later.

Thanks for listening to me. It means a lot. Honest.
Now let's end this book with a hug.

*HUG*

(\ _ /)
(^ x ^ )
c(")(")

## Photo Credits

**Cover photo** — Christine Urias. I have exclusive rights to use it so no funny business, people!

**Chapter 1** — Photo inset of Fonzie/Henry Winkler: public domain (ABC Television). I have no idea who took the school photo of me. If it's you, let me know and I'll send you a cookie in thanks.

**Chapter 2** — Noah's Ark Painting: incredibly talented artist & illustrator, as well as super fun friend, TJ Lubrano

**Chapter 3** — Fancy Meal (Facebook inset): public domain (Peggy Greb, U.S. Department of Agriculture)

**Chapter 4** — Our wedding photo: Photography by Ebert, Oak Park, Illinois (P.S. They're still in business and are still totally awesome, so I'm giving them a plug. Check them out!)

**Chapter 5** — Dad on Ronald Reagan's lap: Northtown News, Chicago, Illinois (August, 1951) Thanks to my Aunt Margie for digitizing it!

**Chapter 7** — McCall's pattern: McCall's ® M7670 Image courtesy of the McCall Pattern Company copyright @2013

**Chapter 9** — That ugly hag is my mom. Man, she was such a good sport. I own the photos but wanted you to know my mom is actually gorgeous with no wrinkles so my brother, Jim, whipped up some Photoshop magic. YIKES!

**Chapter 11** — Darth Vader gargoyle: You caught me in a lie! When we visited the cathedral I tried to take a photo of the gargoyle but failed. Cyraxote to the rescue! public domain (Cyraxote via Wikimedia Commons)
Mamie Eisenhower: White House photo, public domain

All other photographs are mine or stolen from our family archives. Mwa ha ha ha!

## Acknowledgements

Okay, I just wrote a book and spent considerable time crafting a wonderful acknowledgements page. Unfortunately, most of the same people who helped me with *that* book also helped me with *this*. So instead of getting all mushy-gushy, I'm just going to list them. Here they are (drum roll, please):

My fabulous critique partners: Leslie, Sue, and Kim
My fabulous family: Rick, as well as my kids, fictionally known as Peter, Paul and Mary
My fabulous parents: Ted and Janene
My fabulous mother-in-law: Jackie
My fabulous brother and sister-in-law: Jim and Lori
My fabulous friends: Karen and Janette

There is, however, one new addition to the list: my fabulous brother-in-law, Dave.

When Rick and I first met Dave twenty odd years ago, I must admit I wasn't sure about him. He was from Texas, which concerned me. Would he marry my sister, throw her over the back of some horse and take her far, far away?

Then he won us over. The four of us -- me, Rick, Heather, and Dave -- were crossing a busy street in Bloomington, IN. At a break in the traffic, Dave took Heather's hand and bolted across the street screaming in a silly voice, "Run away! Run away!"

Well, if you're a Monty Python fan you'll understand why he stole our hearts right then and there. If you're not, I strongly encourage you to watch one of the greatest movies of all time, *Monty Python's Holy Grail*.

Killer rabbit! ARGH!!!

## About the Author

Originally from the suburbs of Chicago, Illinois, Janene Murphy currently lives in Iowa with her husband and three kids. Her website, www.momsarefrommars.com, reaches readers in over 160 countries. So far, she has published one other book -- a young adult fantasy called *Extraordinary: Light vs. Dark*. She promises to get moving on the sequel to that now that this book is done.

Made in the USA
San Bernardino, CA
05 May 2013